Judaism and
Global Survival

Judaism and Global Survival

Richard H. Schwartz, Ph.D.

VANTAGE PRESS
New York / Washington / Atlanta
Los Angeles / Chicago

Published by Vantage Press, Inc.
516 West 34th Street, New York, New York 10001

Manufactured in the United States of America
ISBN: 533-06045-1

Library of Congress Catalog Card No.: 83-91438

To my dear parents,
Rose and Joseph Schwartz,
for their constant devotion, understanding,
and encouragement

Contents

Prepublication Endorsements

Richard Schwartz's book represents a generous, humane spirit. It is filled with examples of Judaism as a living guide to contemporary life. It says that Jews need only look into their own religious faith and history to discover that all people, not only Jews, are worthy of our concern—and, as Schwartz writes, "Each of us must be Jonah, with a mission to warn the world that it must turn from greed, injustice and idolatry to avoid global oblivion."

Judaism and Global Survival is rich in the teachings of Judaism and reflective of the extraordinarily ethical and moral way of life that has always made us distinctive. It is an important book.

Murray Polner
Editor, *Present Tense*

This masterful volume by Dr. Richard Schwartz provides a treasure of insights into the perspective of Judaism on many urgent social problems. People committed to the vital force of the Jewish heritage will discover in this work both richness of expression and creative application of old texts to new situations. This volume can make a significant contribution to the shaping of the social consciousness of our community.

Rabbi Saul J. Berman
Lincoln Square Synagogue
Professor of Jewish Studies
Stern College of Yeshiva University

. . . Superb task of research, compilation, and writing. . . . [This] book brings to bear scholarly insight which is accessible to the interested lay person. The insights and the values of the Jewish tradition regarding crucial social issues of our time come alive in . . . [this] presentation. Whether used as a textbook or as a personal guide for Jews who care about making Jewish values live in our world, this book makes a significant contribution to the modern understanding of Jewish social justice.

> Rabbi David Saperstein
> Codirector and Counsel
> Religious Action Center
> Commission on Social
>   Action of Reform Judaism

This book is a rich compendium of Jewish sources and ethical insights, and should stimulate many dialogues in the Jewish community about critical issues. One need not agree with all the author's offerings (I disagree with the views on capitalism and national defense, among others) in order to eat of this feast of Jewish values and treasures which are spread before us.

> Rabbi Irving Greenberg
> Director, National Jewish Resource Center

Dr. Schwartz's erudition and moral passion are admirable, as well as his ability to deal with so many subjects so readably and succinctly.

> Dr. Andre Ungar
> Rabbi, Temple Emanuel
> Woodcliff Lake, New Jersey

Preface

I call heaven and earth to witness concerning you this day, that I have set before thee life and death, the blessing and the curse; therefore choose life, that thou mayest live, thou and thy seed.
—Deuteronomy 30:19

The Torah exhorts us to "choose life," but in many ways the world today is choosing death:

- There are now over 50,000 nuclear weapons in the world. The U.S. and the Soviet Union can destroy each other many times over. The world is becoming increasingly insecure as the superpowers move toward first-strike capability and as more and more nations gain the ability to explode nuclear weapons.
- While enough food is being produced to provide an adequate diet for all the world's people, waste, greed, and unjust systems of production and distribution result in millions of deaths annually due to hunger and its effects.
- While the lives of people in wealthy countries are threatened by problems related to overconsumption and waste, half the people on earth lack adequate food, shelter, clean water, education, sanitary facilities, and employment.
- The world's prime ecosystems are endangered, many lakes and streams have been destroyed by acid rain, and many of the world's people are threatened by pesticides and toxic wastes.
- Competition for increasingly scarce resources, such as energy, makes local conflicts and global war more likely.

There is a need for radical changes if the world is to survive. Albert Einstein stated about the nuclear age: "The unleashed power of the atom has changed everything except our modes of thinking, and thus we drift toward unparalleled catastrophe.[1] Economist Kenneth E. Boulding has indicated: "If the human race is to survive it will have to change more in its ways of thinking in the next twenty-five years than it has done in the last twenty-five thousand."[2]

This book is designed to show that we don't need to discover new values and approaches; what is needed is a rediscovery of basic Jewish teachings and mandates, such as to seek and pursue peace, to pursue justice, to love our neighbors as ourselves, and to act as co-workers with God in protecting and preserving the world. We will consider how the *application* of Jewish values can help reduce global crises such as the nuclear arms race, ecological crisis, hunger, poverty, energy shortages, and rapid population growth.

The powerful role that Judaism must play in helping to solve current problems was eloquently expressed by Rabbi Abraham Joshua Heschel, a leading twentieth-century Jewish theologian: "Our civilization is in need of redemption. The evil, the falsehood, the vulgarity of our way of living cry to high heaven. There is a war to be waged against the vulgar, against the glorification of power; a war that is incessant, universal. There is much purification that needs to be done, ought to be done, and could be done through bringing to bear the radical wisdom, the sacrificial devotion, the uncompromising loyalty of our forefathers upon the issues of our daily living."[3]

Recently some Jews, also claiming to base their positions on Jewish teachings, have advocated politically conservative views: increased expenditures for armaments, expanded production of nuclear energy, less assistance from society for poor and hungry people, blind adherence to American foreign policies, to name a few. I believe that these positions miss the major thrust of Jewish values and tradition. They are based on considerations of "Realpolitik" rather than Jewish prophetic teachings, and mistakenly perceive both Judaism and the demands of global survival.

Unfortunately, instead of the Judaism of the prophets and sages, with its passionate concern for justice, peace, and righteousness, we often see in our community today what we might call "establishment Judaism." There is little active involvement, few protests against injustice, and much complacency and conformity. Establishment Judaism has in many instances made peace with the powers that be; it worships modern idols of materialism, state power, technology, fame, empty rituals, personal ambition, and overconsumption. The radical messages of the Torah and the prophets have been suppressed. Establishment Judaism has forgotten the mandate not to conform to the world, but to radically transform it. Today the synagogues and pronouncements of rabbis have frequently become irrelevant to the critical problems that face the world's people. God requires justice, compassion, involvement, and protests against evil, but our synagogues have too often focused on ritual and parochial concerns.

A person who takes Jewish values seriously would be alienated by much of what goes on in Jewish life today. As Rabbi Heschel stated, "One is embarrassed to be called religious in the face of religion's failure to keep alive the image of God in the face of man." Many idealistic Jews have turned away from Judaism because of its failure to be involved in today's crucial issues.

For Jews, the act of helping the needy and caring for the world is not a voluntary option but a responsibility, a divine command. It is not only an individual responsibility, but an obligation for the whole society. Our tradition understands this as a covenant—an agreement that binds us to God. In this covenant, we assume the task of repairing the world and in return receive the divine promise that the world will be redeemed. The Jewish message is not only one of responsibility, but also one of hope.

It is a shame that some Jewish leaders and institutions have for- ·gotten that the practical expression of justice, in our own community and toward all communities, has been and must continue to be the major emphasis of Jewish living. We cannot allow whatever other legitimate needs or fears that we may have to take us away from our own Jewish values.

It is also unfortunate that many searching Jews are unaware of the rich legacy of the Jewish tradition and its focus on justice for both the individual and society. Judaism indeed provides a pragmatic path for implementing its progressive ideas. The entire Talmudic and Rabbinic tradition is full of lengthy discussion, advice, and legal decisions on how to apply the principles of the prophets to situations in everyday life. As well, Judaism offers the richness and warmth of an ancient historic community, a meaningful inheritance for each Jew.

This book is not meant to be a complete analysis of all current critical problems nor of all Jewish positions. It does not attempt to give all sides of every issue. It does try to show that Judaism demands passionate concern and involvement in society's problems and protest against the current policies that are increasing poverty and hunger, wasting natural resources, threatening ecosystems, causing rapid population growth, and, most important, increasing the chances of global nuclear holocaust.

It is hoped that this book will help start a dialogue on Jewish teachings concerning critical issues and that it will play a part in moving our precious planet away from its present path toward annihilation.

Acknowledgments

In order to get a broader perspective on the many issues, Jewish and secular, considered in this book, I consulted with many people with widely varying views. While every comment on the early drafts was helpful, the suggestions of the following individuals were especially valuable: Ben Abelow, Edward Aberlin, Joseph Adler, Rabbi Philip Bentley, Aviva Cantor, Professor Seymour Finger, Professor Joseph Fishman, Rabbi Martin Garfinkle, Sally Gladstein, Robert Greenberg, Rabbi Fishel Hochbaum, Sister Maura Hyland, Rabbi Marcus Kramer, Murray Polner, Edward Rothberg, Rabbi Jeffrey Rappoport, Steven Schwartz, David Seidenberg, Rabbi Gerry Serotta, Alan Solomonow, Rabbi Andre Ungar, and Rabbi Noach Valley. Special thanks to Jeff Oboler, director of the Martin Steinberg Center, for his many constructive comments and his valuable material for the preface.

Sincere gratitude is especially owed to Jonathan Wolf, a dedicated Jewish activist, for reviewing the entire final manuscript and for making many constructive suggestions.

Deep appreciation is expressed to Rabbi Yaakov Marcus, spiritual leader of the Young Israel of Staten Island, whose excellent classes and sermons provided much "food-for-thought" on the issues considered in this book.

Although these people have been very helpful, the author takes full responsibility for the final selection of material and interpretations.

I wish to thank Caryl Reines Herzfeld for her excellent artwork, which served as the basis for the cover design of this book, and Shelly Berger, who created the final cover.

Appreciation is due to George Platt, who took the author's photograph.

Thanks also to the reprographics staff at the College of Staten Island for their help in assembling the drafts of this book: Jay Blum, Larry McLoughlin, Michael Metz, David Poignant, and Eugene Rasmussen.

I wish to express sincere appreciation to my wife, Loretta, and our children, Susan, David, and Deborah, for their patience, understanding, and encouragement. They made valuable suggestions and were with me through every stage of this work.

Finally, I wish to thank in advance all who will read this book and send me ideas and suggestions for improvements so that it can better lead toward that day when Jewish values are applied toward the creation of a safe, sane, more just world.

*Judaism and
Global Survival*

Chapter 1

Involvement and Protest

Whoever is able to protest against the transgressions of his own family and does not do so is punished for the transgressions of his family. Whoever is able to protest against the transgressions of the people of his community and does not do so is punished for the transgressions of his community. Whoever is able to protest against the transgressions of the entire world and does not do so is punished for the transgressions of the entire world.

—Shabbat 54b

Judaism urges involvement in issues facing society. A Jew must not be concerned only about his own personal affairs while the community is in trouble:

> If a man of learning participates in public affairs and serves as judge or arbiter, he gives stability to the land. But if he sits in his home and says to himself, "What have the affairs of society to do with me? . . . Why should I trouble myself with the people's voices of protest? Let my soul dwell in peace!"—if he does this, he overthrows the world.
>
> Tanchuma to Mishpatim

Judaism teaches that people must struggle for the good society. The Torah frequently admonishes: "And thou shalt eradicate the evil from your midst" (Deuteronomy 13:6, 17:7, 21:21, 24:7). Injustice cannot be accepted; it must be actively resisted and, ultimately, eliminated. The Talmudic sages taught that Jerusalem was destroyed because its citizens failed in their responsibility to criticize one another (Shabbat 99b). They indicated that "Love which does not contain the element of criticism is not really love" (Genesis Rabbah 54:3).

Many people think of religion in terms of adherence to rituals, study, and prayer. But, as indicated in the following Midrash (a story based on Biblical events that illustrates rabbinic values), to be con-

1

sidered pious, a person must protest against injustice. Even God is challenged to apply this standard in judging people.

> R. Acha ben R. Chanina said: Never did a favorable word go forth from the mouth of the Holy One which He retracted for evil, save the following: "And the Lord said to His angel: 'Go through the city, through Jerusalem, and put a mark upon the foreheads of the men who sigh and groan over all the abominations that are committed there' " (Ezekiel 9:4). (Thus, they will be protected from the angels who are slaying the wicked.)
>
> At that moment, the indignant prosecutor came forward in the Heavenly Court.
>
> Prosecutor: Lord, wherein are these (marked ones) different from those (the rest)?
>
> God: These are wholly righteous men, while those are wholly wicked.
>
> Prosecutor: But Lord, they had the power to protest, but did not.
>
> God: It was known to Me that had they protested, they would not have been heeded.
>
> Prosecutor: But Lord, if it was revealed to Thee, was it revealed to them? Accordingly, they should have protested and incurred scorn for thy holy Name, and have been ready to suffer blows . . . as did the prophets suffer from Israel.
>
> God revoked his original order, and the righteous were found guilty, because of their failure to protest.
>
> Shabbat 55a, Tanchuma Tazria 9

It is not sufficient merely to do good deeds while acquiescing in unjust conditions. The Maharal of Prague, a sixteenth-century Jewish philosopher, stated that individual piety pales in the face of the sin of not protesting against an emerging communal evil, and a person will be held accountable for not preventing wickedness when capable of doing so.[1]

One major problem with silence in the face of evil is that it implies acceptance or possibly even support. According to Rabbenu Yonah, a medieval ethicist, sinners may think to themselves, "Since others are neither reproving nor contending against us, our deeds are permissible."[2]

Rabbi Joachim Prinz, a refugee from pre–World War II Nazi Germany and former president of the American Jewish Congress, told 200,000 people who marched on Washington in 1963 on behalf of human freedom that under Hitler's rule, he had learned about the problem of apathy toward fellow human beings: ". . . bigotry and hatred are not the most urgent problem. The most urgent, the most disgraceful, the most shameful and most tragic problem is silence."[3]

Rabbi Abraham Joshua Heschel believed that apathy to injustice results in greater wickedness. He stated that "indifference to evil is more insidious than evil itself" and that silent acquiescence leads to evil being accepted and becoming the rule.[4]

Jews are required to protest and try to make changes even when it appears futile. The Talmudic sage R. Zera taught that "Even though people will not accept it, you should rebuke them" (Shabbat 55a). We can never be sure that our words and actions will be ineffective. Thus the only responsible approach is to exert our best efforts. In the Mishna's famous formulation:

> It is not your obligation to complete the task. But neither are you free to desist from it.
>
> Pirke Avot 2:21

Just as many drops of water can carve a hole in a rock, many small efforts can become a major influence.

There are times when a person must continue to protest in order to avoid being corrupted:

> A man stood at the entrance of Sodom crying out against the injustice and evil in that city. Someone passed by and said to him, "For years you have been urging the people to repent, and yet no one has changed. Why do you continue?" He responded: "When I first came, I protested because I hoped to change the people of Sodom. Now I continue to cry out, because if I don't, they will have changed me."

In his excellent article "The Rabbinic Ethics of Protest," Rabbi Reuven Kimelman indicates that the means of protest must be consistent with responsibility to the community. He states that love and truth must be involved, where love implies the willingness to suffer and truth the willingness to resist. Together, he concludes, they point to nonviolent resistance, toward the ends of justice and peace.[5]

The Talmud teaches that controversy and protest must be "for the sake of Heaven" (Pirke Avot 5:20). The protest of Korach against the rule of Moses in the wilderness (Numbers 16:1–35) is considered negatively by the Jewish tradition because it was based on jealousy and personal motives.

3

Protest in Jewish History

From its beginning, Judaism has often protested against greed, injustice, and misused power. Abraham, the first Jew, smashed the idols of his father at great personal risk. He established the precedent that a Jew should not conform to society's values when they are evil. Later he even challenged God, exclaiming, "Shall not the Judge of all the earth do justly?" (Genesis 18:25). By contrast, Noah, though righteous personally, was later rebuked by the Talmudic sages because he failed to criticize the immorality of his society. Even before assuming leadership of the Jewish people, Moses became involved in battling injustice and seeking reconciliation. He slew an Egyptian who was oppressing a Jew, attempted to halt fighting between two Jews, and aided Jethro's daughters (non-Jews) when they were being harassed by shepherds in Midian.

Balaam, the biblical pagan prophet, intended to curse Israel but ended up blessing them: "Lo, it is a people dwelling alone, and not reckoning itself among the nations" (Numbers 23:9). To the Israelites, the keynote of their existence was "I am the Lord your God, who has separated you from the peoples that you should be Mine" (Leviticus 20:26). Throughout their history, Jews have often been nonconformists who refused to acquiesce in the false values of the surrounding community.

When the Jews were in Persia, Mordecai refused to defer to an evil ruler. As the book of Esther states: ". . . And all the king's servants . . . bowed down and prostrated themselves before Haman. . . . But Mordecai would not bow down nor prostrate himself before him" (Esther 3:2). Mordecai felt that bowing down to a human being was inconsistent with his obligation to worship only God. Later Mordecai condemned inaction in urging Esther to take risks to save the Jewish people (Esther 4:13,14).

The greatest champions of protest against unjust conditions were the Hebrew prophets. Rabbi Abraham Heschel summarized the attributes of these spokesmen for God: They had the ability to hold God and people in one thought, at one time; they could not be tranquil in an unjust world; they were supremely impatient with evil, due to their intense sensitivity to God's concern for right and wrong; they were advocates for those too weak to plead their own cause (the widow, the orphan, the oppressed); their major activity was interference, remonstrating against wrongs inflicted on other people.[6]

Today we generally have a relatively moderate reaction to immoral acts. We try to strike a happy medium while there is extreme agony for the oppressed. But not so the prophets:

> Cry aloud, spare not,
> Lift up your voice like a trumpet,
> And declare unto My people their transgression, . . .
> Is this not the fast that I have chosen?
> To loose the bonds of wickedness,
> To undo the thongs of the yoke,
> To let the oppressed go free,
> And to break every yoke.
>
> Isaiah 58:1,6

The prophet Amos berated those who were content amidst destruction and injustice (6:1,4–6):

> Woe to those who are at ease in Zion,
> And to those who feel secure on the mountains of Samaria, . . .
> Woe to those who lie upon beds of ivory,
> And stretch themselves upon their couches,
> And eat lambs from the flock,
> And calves from the midst of the stall;
> Who sing idle songs to the sound of the harp, . . .
> Who drink wine in bowls,
> And anoint themselves in the finest oils,
> But are not grieved on the ruin of Joseph!

In order to carry out their role, to be a kingdom of priests and a light unto the nations, Jews throughout history found it necessary to live in the world, but apart from it—in effect, on the other side. This, the sages commented, was implied in the very name "Hebrew" (*ivri*), from *"ever,"* the other side: "The whole world was on one side [idolators] and he [Abraham, the Hebrew] was on the other side" (Genesis Rabbah). Jacques Maritain, a French Catholic philosopher, wrote in 1939 that the Jewish people were

> found at the very heart of the world's structure, stimulating it, exasperating it, moving it. . . It [the Jewish people] gives the world no peace, it bars slumber, it teaches the world to be discontented and restless as long as the world has not accepted God.[7]

Based on Jewish tradition and values, Jews have been active in many protest movements. Some of these movements have been primarily Jewishly oriented such as the struggles for Soviet Jewry and, more recently, for Ethiopian Jewry. But Jews have also been prominent in protests for a cleaner environment, for a more peaceful world, and for human rights. A group of rabbis, acting in accordance with the Jewish ethic of protest, explained why they came to St. Augustine, Florida, in 1964 to demonstrate against segregation in that community:

> We came because we could not stand silently by our brother's blood. We had done that too many times before. We have been vocal in our exhortation of others but the idleness of our hands too often revealed an inner silence. . . . We came as Jews who remember the millions of faceless people who stood quietly, watching the smoke rise from Hitler's crematoria. We came because we know that second only to silence, the greatest danger to man is loss of faith in man's capacity to act.[8]

The Current Lack of Protest

Religious practitioners have often distorted God's demands. Instead of crying out against immorality, injustice, deceit, cruelty, and violence, they frequently condoned these evils, while emphasizing ceremonies and ritual. To many Jews today, Judaism involves occasional visits to the synagogue or temple, prayers recited with little feeling, rituals performed with little meaning, and socializing. But, to the prophets worship along with indifference to evil is an absurdity, an abomination to God.[9] Judaism is mocked when Jews indulge in or condone immoral deeds.

While ritual is important, God's primary concern for justice is powerfully expressed by the prophet Amos (5:22–24):

> Even though you offer Me your burnt offerings and cereal
>   offerings,
> I will not accept them,
> And the peace offerings of your fatted beasts
> I will not look upon.
> Take away from Me the noise of your songs;
> To the melody of your harps I will not listen.
> But let justice well up as waters,
> And righteousness as a mighty stream.

The prophet Hosea (6:6) similarly states God's preference for moral and spiritual dedication rather than outward ritual:

> For I desire kindness and not sacrifice,
> Attachment to God rather than burnt offerings.

Yet all too often today Jews have failed to speak out against an unjust, immoral society. While claiming to follow the ethical teachings of the prophets, many Jews have equivocated and rationalized inaction. Rabbi Heschel blames religion's failure to speak out and be involved in critical current issues for its losses:

> Religion declined not because it was refuted but because it became irrelevant, dull, oppressive, insipid. When faith is completely replaced by habit, when the crisis of today is ignored because of the splendor of the past, when faith becomes an heirloom rather than a living fountain, when religion speaks only in the name of authority rather than with the voice of compassion, its message becomes meaningless.[10]

The Gesher Foundation is a highly respected Israeli group that has been striving to build a *gesher* (bridge) between religious and nonreligious Israeli youth. It has stated that its task has been made more difficult by the lack of involvement of the Israeli religious community in ethical issues:

> Why do we not discern any special ethical sensitivity among religious people? Why does the religious community not stand at the forefront of the war against social ills? How can the religious community remain cloistered within its narrow four cubits when the moral fabric of society is being rent without?[11]

Unfortunately, the same questions are relevant to the diaspora Jewish community as well. Many idealistic Jews are turned off to Judaism by the lack of involvement and moral commitment which they find in Jewish religious institutions. Rabbi Abraham Karp, who taught at Dartmouth College in the 1960s, felt that students would only be attracted to a "church or synagogue which dares, which challenges, which disturbs, which acts as a critic, which leads in causes which are moral."[12] Reinhold Niebuhr, the widely respected Christian theologian, related religion's failure to attract idealistic people to their failure to protest injustice. He stated that the chief reason that many people turn from religion is that the "social impotence of religion outrages their conscience."[13]

7

Many Jews today justify their lack of involvement with the world's problems by stating that Jews have enough troubles of their own and that others can work on "non-Jewish" issues. Certainly Jews should be involved in battling anti-Semitism, working for a secure Israel, and other Jewish issues. But can we divorce ourselves from concern about more general problems? Are they really "non-Jewish" issues? Don't Jews also suffer from polluted air and water, unemployment, inflation, and resource shortages? If a nuclear war did occur, would Jews be spared?

Perhaps the situation is, in mathematical terms, like a problem in conditional probability. If conditions in the world are good, it is still possible that Jews will suffer. But if these conditions are bad, it is almost *certain* that Jews will be negatively affected. Hence, even considering self-interest alone, Jews must be involved in working for a just and harmonious world.

It is essential that Jews actively apply Jewish values to current critical problems. We must be God's loyal opposition on earth, rousing the conscience of humanity. We must shout NO when others are whispering yes to injustice. We must restore Judaism to the task of "comforting the afflicted and afflicting the comfortable." We must act as befits "descendants of prophets" (Pesachim 66b), reminding the world that there is a God of justice, compassion, and kindness. Nothing less than global survival is at stake.

As the following chapters will show, the world is rapidly plunging toward disaster due to its failure to take religious values seriously. It is hoped that, once informed, Jews and others will get involved and protest to help save the world before it is too late.

Chapter 2

Human Rights and Obligations

> *One person (Adam) was created as the common ancestor of all, for the sake of the peace of the human race, so that one should not be able to say to a neighbor, "My ancestor was better than yours."*
>
> *One person was created to teach us the sanctity and importance of every life, for "he who destroys one life, it is as if he destroys an entire world, and he who saves one life, it is as if he saves an entire world!"*
>
> *One person was created to teach us the importance of the actions of every individual, for "we should treat the world as half good and half bad, so that if we do one good deed, it will tip the whole world to the side of goodness."*
>
> —Mishna Sanhedrin 4:5

A fundamental Jewish principle is the equality and unity of humanity. We all have one Father; one God has created everyone. Judaism is a universal religion that condemns discrimination based on race, color, or nationality. Every person is endowed with equal rights.

The lesson of universality inherent in the creation of one common ancestor is reinforced by the following teaching of the sages: "God formed Adam out of dust from all over the world: yellow clay, white sand, black loam, and red soil. Therefore, no one can declare to any race or color of people that they do not belong here since this soil is not their home" (Yalkut Shimoni 1:13). Hence Adam represents every person.

This concept is also reinforced by Ben Azzai, a disciple of Rabbi Akiva. He states that a great, fundamental teaching of the Torah is the verse "This is the book of the generations of MAN (*adam*)" (Genesis 5:1). The statement does not talk about black, or white, or Jew, or Gentile, but MAN. Since all human beings have a common ancestor, they must necessarily be brothers and sisters. Hence these words proclaim the essential message that there is a unity to the human race.

Imitation of God's Ways

One of the most important ideas related to the creation of humanity is that "God created man in His own image; in the image of God created He him; male and female created He them." (Genesis 1:27). According to a Talmudic rabbi, "Beloved is man, for he was created in the image of God" (Pirke Avot 3:18). In the following Biblical verse, the Torah mandates that we walk in God's ways:

> For if ye shall diligently keep all this commandment which I command you to do it, to love the Lord thy God, to walk in all His ways, and to cleave to Him, . . .
>
> Deuteronomy11:22

The Midrash interprets the expression "walking in God's ways" to mean "Just as He is called 'merciful,' be thou merciful, just as He is called 'compassionate,' be thou compassionate" (Sifre to Deuteronomy 11:22).

The idea of the imitation of God is also based on the well-known verse in the Holiness code: "Ye shall be holy, for I, the Lord thy God, am holy" (Leviticus 19:2).

The third-century Palestinian teacher Hama ben Hanina expands on the duty of imitating God:

> What is the meaning of the verse "Ye shall walk after the Lord thy God" (Deut. 13:5)? Is it possible for a human being to walk after the *Shechinah* (God's presence), for has it not been said, "For the Lord thy God is a devouring fire" (Deut. 4:24)? But the verse means to walk after the attributes of the Holy One, Blessed is He. As He clothes the naked, for it is written, "And the Lord God made for Adam and his wife coats of skin and clothed them" (Genesis 3:21), so do thou clothe the naked. The Holy One, Blessed is He, visited the sick, for it is written, "And the Lord appeared to him (Abraham, while he was recovering from circumcision), by the oaks of Mamre" (Genesis 18:1), so do thou also visit the sick. The Holy One, Blessed is He, comforted mourners, for it is written, "And it came to pass after the death of Abraham, that God blessed Isaac, his son" (Genesis 25:11), so do thou comfort mourners. The Holy One, Blessed is He, buried the dead, for it

is written, "And He buried him in the valley" (Deut. 34:6), so do thou also bury the dead.

Sotah 14a

Maimonides finds a powerful statement about the importance of imitating God in these words from the prophet Jeremiah:

Thus says the Lord:
Let not the wise man glory in his wisdom;
Neither let the mighty man glory in his might;
Let not the rich man glory in his riches;
But let him that glories, glory in this:
That he understands and knows Me,
That I am the Lord who exercises mercy, justice, and
    righteousness, on the earth;
For in these things I delight, says the Lord.

Jeremiah 9:22–23

Maimonides interpreted this statement to mean that a person should find fulfillment in the imitation of God, in being "like God in his actions."[1] He turned from his path of writing based on contemplation of God to what he came to consider a person's ultimate end: the copying of God's traits of kindness, justice, and righteousness. He renounced his former practice of seclusion and ministered to the sick throughout each day (as a physician).[2]

While Judaism has many beautiful symbols, such as the mezuzah, menorah, and sukkah, there is only one symbol that represents God, and that is each person. As Rabbi Abraham Joshua Heschel has taught, "more important than to have a symbol is to be a symbol." And every person can consider himself or herself as a symbol of God. This is our challenge: to live in a way compatible with being a symbol of God, to walk in God's ways, to remember who we are and Whom we represent, and to remember our role as partners of God in working to redeem the world.

Love of Neighbor

A central commandment in Judaism is "Thou shalt love thy neighbor as thyself" (Leviticus 19:18). According to Rabbi Akiva, this is the great principle of the Torah. Rabbi Levi Yitzhak of Berditschev said: "whether a man really loves God can be determined by the love he bears toward his fellow man."[3]

There is some controversy as to whether this should be applied only to fellow Jews or all humanity. Rabbi J. H. Hertz, former chief rabbi of England, states that the translation of the Hebrew word *rea* (neighbor) as "fellow Israelite" is incorrect. He cites several examples in the Torah where that word means "neighbor of whatever race or creed."[4]

The commandment "Love thy neighbor as thyself" logically follows from the Jewish principle that each person has been created in God's image. Hence, since my neighbor is like myself, I should love him as myself. In fact, the proper translation of the commandment is "Love thy neighbor; he is like thyself."

The sages in the Talmud spell out how one should love a human being:

> One should practice loving-kindness *(gemilut chasadim)*, not only by giving of one's possessions, but by personal effort on behalf of one's fellowman, such as extending a free loan, visiting the sick, offering comfort to mourners and attending weddings. For alms giving *(tzedakah)* there is the minimum of the tithe (one-tenth) and the maximum of one-fifth of one's income. But there is no fixed measure of personal service.
>
> Mishnah Peah I

Rabbi Moshe Leib of Sassov tells us how to love our neighbor as ourself through relating an experience in his life:

> How to love men is something I learned from a peasant. He was sitting in an inn along with the other peasants, drinking. . . he asked one of the men seated beside him: "Tell me, do you love me or don't you love me?" The other replied, "I love you very much." The first peasant nodded his head, was silent for a while, then remarked: "You say that you love me, but you do not know what I need. If you really loved me, you should know." The other had not a word to say to this, and the peasant who put the question fell again silent. But I understood. To know the needs of men and to bear the burden of their sorrow—that is the true love of man.[5]

Aaron, the brother of Moses, also teaches how we can love our neighbors. When two people were quarreling, he would go to each separately and tell them how the other deeply regretted their argument and wished reconciliation. When the two would next meet, they would often embrace and reestablish friendly relations. Because of such acts of love and kindness by Aaron, Hillel exhorts people to

> Be of the disciples of Aaron, loving peace and pursuing peace, loving humanity, and drawing them closer to the Torah.
>
> Pirke Avot 1:12

When Hillel was confronted by a pagan who demanded that the sage explain all of the Torah while standing on one leg, his response was similar to "Love thy neighbor as thyself": "What is hateful to you, do not do unto others,—that is the entire Torah; everything else is commentary. Go and learn." (Shabbat 31a).

Kindness to Strangers

To further emphasize that "love of neighbor" applies to every human being, the Torah frequently commands that we show love and consideration for the stranger, "for you know the heart of the stranger, seeing that you were strangers in the land of Egypt" (Exodus 23:9).

The stranger was one who came from distant parts of the land of Israel or, like the immigrants of our own day, from a foreign country. The Torah stresses the importance of treating them with respect and empathy.

The importance placed on the commandment not to mistreat the stranger in our midst is indicated by its appearance thirty-six times in the Torah, far more than any other *mitzvah*.[6] It is placed on the same level as the duty of kindness to and protection of the widow and the orphan.[7] [The Talmud and rabbinic tradition understand most of these references to the 'stranger' to refer to those who convert to Judaism (*ger tzedek*) or to non-Jews living in the land of Israel who accept Jewish sovereignty and observe basic laws of morality (*ger toshav*).] Hermann Cohen stated that true religion began with the concept of shielding the alien from all wrong. He commented:

> The alien was to be protected, although he was not a member of one's family, clan, religious community, or people; simply because he was a human being. In the alien, therefore, man discovered the idea of humanity.[8]

In today's world, with its great clannishness and nationalism, with its often harsh treatment of people who don't share the local religion, nationality, or culture, the Torah's teachings about the stranger are remarkable:

> And a stranger shalt thou not wrong, neither shalt thou oppress him; for ye were strangers in the land of Egypt.
> Exodus 22:20; Leviticus 19:33

> Love ye therefore the stranger; for ye were strangers in the land of Egypt.
> Deuteronomy 10:19; Leviticus 19:34

13

> And thou shalt rejoice in all the good which the Lord, thy God hath given thee . . . and the stranger that is in the midst of thee.
>
> Deuteronomy 26:11

The stranger is guaranteed the same protection in the law court and in payment of wages as the native:

> Judge righteously between a man and his brother and the stranger that is with him.
>
> Deuteronomy 1:16

> Thou shalt not oppress a hired servant that is poor and needy, whether he be of thy brethren, or of the strangers that are in thy land within thy gates. In the same day thou shalt give him his hire.
>
> Deuteronomy 24:14,15

When it comes to divine forgiveness, the stranger stands on an equal footing with the native:

> And all the congregation of the children of Israel shall be forgiven and the stranger that sojourneth among them.
>
> Numbers 15:26

Like any other needy person, the stranger had free access to the grain that was to be left unharvested in the corners of the field and to the gleanings of the harvest, as well as to fallen grapes or odd clusters of grapes remaining on the vine after picking (Leviticus 19:9,10; 23:22; Deuteronomy 24:21). The stranger, like the widow and the fatherless, was welcome to the forgotten sheaves in the fields (Deuteronomy 24:19) and olives clinging to the beaten trees (Deuteronomy 24:20). He also partook of the tithe (the tenth part of the produce) every third year of the Sabbatical cycle (Deuteronomy 14:28,29; 26:12) and was able to join in the rejoicing connected with Shavuot (Deuteronomy 16:10–12), and Sukkot (Deuteronomy 16:13,14).[9]

Treatment of Non-Jews

Since God is the Father of all people, every human being is entitled to proper treatment. A person's actions, and not his or her faith or creed, is most important, as indicated in the following Talmudic teachings:

> I bring heaven and earth to witness that the Holy Spirit dwells upon a non-Jew as well as upon a Jew, upon a woman as well as upon a man, upon maid-servant as well as man-servant. All depend on the deeds of the particular individual!
>
> Yalkut to Judges 4:4 from *Tanna de Vei Eliyahu*

> In all nations, there are righteous individuals who will have a share in the world to come.
>
> Tosefta Sanhedrin 13:2

The Talmud contains many statutes that safeguard the rights of non-Jews.

> We support the poor of the heathen along with the poor of Israel and visit the sick of the heathen along with the sick of Israel and bury the dead of the heathen along with the dead of Israel, for the sake of peace. . . .
>
> Gittin 61a

> In a city where there are both Jews and Gentile, the collectors of alms collect from both Jews and Gentiles; they feed the poor of both, visit the sick of both, bury both, comfort the mourners whether they be Jews or Gentiles, and restore the lost goods of both, for the sake of peace.
>
> Yerushalmi Demai 4:6 (24a)

Because of cruel treatment by non-Jews during many periods, certain discriminatory laws against gentiles were instituted at particular times, but the essential spirit of Judaism toward other people was expressed by Maimonides in his Mishneh Torah (18:1):

> Jew and non-Jew are to be treated alike. If a (Jewish) vendor knows that his merchandise is defective, he must inform the purchaser (whatever his religion).

Influenced by this statement by Maimonides, Rabbi Menahem Meiri of Provence ruled in the fourteenth century that a Jew *should* desecrate the Sabbath to save the life of a Gentile.[10] Meiri stated that any previous law to the contrary had been intended only for ancient times for those non-Jews who were violent heathens without a sense of ethical duty to society.[11] This decision was quoted recently by former

15

Israeli chief rabbi Chaim Unterman in a responsum in which he vigorously denied a charge raised by a Dr. Shahak that Jewish law forbids violating the Sabbath to save a gentile's life.[12]

R. Ezekiel Landau ruled in an eighteenth-century responsum:

> I emphatically declare that in all laws contained in the Jewish writings concerning theft, fraud, etc., no distinction is made between Jew and Gentile; that the titles goy, *akum* (idolater), etc., in no wise apply to the people among whom we live.

The following Midrash dramatically shows that Jews are to treat every person (not just fellow Jews) justly:

> Shimeon ben Shetah used to work hard preparing flax. His disciples said to him, "Rabbi, desist. We will buy you an ass, and you will not have to work so hard." They went and bought an ass from an Arab, and a pearl was found on it, whereupon they came to R. Shimeon and said, "From now on you need not work anymore." "Why?" he asked. They said, "We bought you an ass from an Arab, and a pearl was found on it." He said to them, "Does its owner know of that?" They answered, "No." He said to them, "Go and give the pearl back to him." To their argument that he need not return the pearl because the Arab was a heathen, he responded, "Do you think that Shimeon ben Shetah is a barbarian? He would prefer to hear the Arab say, 'Blessed be the God of the Jews,' than possess all the riches of the world. . . . It is written, 'You shall not oppress your neighbor. 'Now your neighbor is as your brother, and your brother is as your neighbor. Hence you learn that to rob a Gentile is robbery."

Deuteronomy Rabbah 3:3

Slavery in the Biblical Period

From today's perspective, the widespread and legalized practice of slavery in biblical times would seem to contradict Jewish values with regard to treatment of human beings. However, we must look at slavery in terms of an evolving process; it was a common practice in ancient times and thought to be an economic necessity. Therefore, the Torah did not outlaw it immediately but, through its teachings and laws, the Torah had the effect of eventually eliminating slavery, to fulfill its desired aim.

Slavery in Israel's early history had many humane features, especially in comparison with practices in other countries. Slaves' rights were guarded and regulated with increasingly humanitarian legislation. They were recognized as having certain inalienable rights based on their humanity. Slaves had to be allowed to rest on the Sabbath Day.

The Talmud proclaimed legislation in order to mitigate slavery's harshness, especially with regard to a Hebrew slave:

> He [the slave] should be with you in food and with you in drink, lest you eat clean bread and he moldy bread, or lest you drink old wine and he new wine, or lest you sleep on soft feathers and he on straw. So it was said, "Whoever buys a Hebrew slave for himself, it is as if he purchased a master for himself."
>
> Kiddushin 20a

It is significant that, unlike the law of the U.S. before the Civil War, the Biblical fugitive-slave law protected the runaway slave:

> Thou shalt not deliver to his master a bondsman that is escaped from his master unto you. He shall dwell with you in the midst of you, in the place which he shall choose within one of your gates, where he likes it best; thou shalt not wrong him.
>
> Deuteronomy 23:16,17

Violations of Human Rights

The test of the decency of a community is in its attitude toward strangers. A good society teaches its members to overcome their fear of outsiders and to be kind to those who are disadvantaged.

Unfortunately, the history of the world is largely a history of the violation of human rights. Today there is widespread discrimination against and even oppression of people of different race, religion, nationality, or economic status. As discussed in chapter 10, due to injustice and repression, half the world's people lack adequate food, shelter, employment, education, health care, clean water, and other basic human needs.

Perhaps no people has historically suffered more from prejudice than Jews. The Crusades, the Inquisition, and the Holocaust are just three of the most horrible examples in our history. Many times Jews have been killed, subjected to pogroms, forced to convert, or exiled from their native land. Whenever conditions were bad, the economy suffered, or there was a plague, local Jews provided a convenient scapegoat.

Anti-Semitism continues today. Many feel that it is getting worse, as Nazi-type groups and the Ku Klux Klan become increasingly active. There are even groups who deny that the Holocaust ever occurred. There are several Jewish groups such as the Anti-Defamation League of B'nai B'rith, which are working to reduce anti-Semitism. Much more needs to be done to eliminate this ancient, scandalous disease.

It is essential to educate all people to the evils of prejudice and anti-Semitism. In addition to openly confronting and opposing the barbarities of anti-Semitism and racism, it is also necessary to work for a healthy America and world, get rid of slums, poverty, hunger, and illiteracy, to provide a decent job and housing and a fair chance at life for everyone, and to strive for justice for oppressed people. A just, democratic society will be far safer for Jews and every other group.

Jewish Views on Racism

An incident in the life of Moses illustrates Judaism's strong condemnation of racial prejudice. Miriam and Aaron spoke against Moses because of the Cushite (black) woman he had married. God was very angry, and He rebuked them for challenging Moses. Miriam was punished by being stricken with leprosy: she turned white as punishment for making color an issue in the treatment of human beings (Numbers 12:1–10).

The prophet Amos challenged the state of mind that looks down on darker-skinned people, in a ringing declaration on the equality of all races and nations. He compared the Jewish people to blacks and indicated that God was even concerned with Israel's enemies, such as the Philistines and Syrians.

> Are ye not as the children of the Ethiopians unto me,
> O children of Israel? saith the Lord.
> Have I not brought up Israel out of the land of Egypt?
> And the Philistines from Caphtor,
> And the Syrians from Kir?
>
> Amos 9:7

A biblical passage often invoked by exponents of black inferiority is an incident in Genesis (9:20–27). After the Flood, Noah planted a vineyard, and, becoming drunk from its fruit, he stripped himself of his clothes in his tent. Noah's son Ham, the father of Canaan, looked on the nakedness of his father and reported it to his brothers, Shem and Japheth. The two brothers covered their father's nakedness without putting him to shame. When Noah awoke from his wine, he learned what Ham had done and declared:

> Cursed be Canaan;
> A servant of servants shall he be unto his brethren.
> And he said, Blessed be the Lord God of Shem;
> And Canaan shall be his servant
> God shall enlarge Japheth,
> And he shall dwell in the tents of Shem;
> And Canaan shall be his servant.
>
> Genesis 9:25–27

Note that it was Canaan, who was entirely guiltless, who was cursed with slavery, rather than Ham (the father of the darker races), who had failed to show proper respect to his father. Perhaps this is because the Bible is more interested in Canaan, since his descendants were conquered by the Israelities. The point is that there is no curse of slavery or inferiority placed upon Ham or his black descendants.

Judaism teaches the sacredness of every person, but this is not what is generally practiced in our society. And, as with many other moral issues, religion has seldom spoken out in protest.

Rabbi Abraham Heschel points out the tremendous threat that racism poses to humanity:

> . . . And racism is worse than idolatry. *Racism is satanism, unmitigated evil.*
>
> Few of us seem to realize how insidious, how radical, how universal an evil racism is. Few of us realize that racism is man's gravest threat to man, the maximum of hatred for a minimum of reason, the maximum of cruelty for a minimum of thinking.[13]

He points out that bigotry is inconsistent with a proper relationship with God:

> Prayer and prejudice cannot dwell in the same heart. Worship without compassion is worse than self-deception; it is an abomination.[14]

He asserts that "what is lacking is a sense of the *monstrosity of inequality*."[15] Consistent with the Jewish view of every person created in God's image, he boldly states: "God is every man's pedigree. He is either the Father of all men or of no men. The image of God is either in every man or in no man."[16]

It is an embarrassing fact that most of our religious institutions did not originally take the lead in proclaiming the evil of segregation; they had to be prodded into action by the decision of the Supreme Court of the United States in the case of *Brown* v. *the Board of Education* in 1954.

Based on Jewish values of compassion and justice, many Jews have been active in the struggle for black rights. Two Jewish college students, Andrew Goodman and Michael Schwerner, were brutally murdered while working for civil rights in Mississippi in 1964. Recently there have been some splits in the Jewish-black coalition due to disagreements on such issues as quotas and Israel. Yet, while some on both sides would emphasize points of disharmony, Jews and blacks have many common interests and goals and have much to gain by working together for a more just, compassionate, peaceful, and harmonious society.

Jewish treatment of disadvantaged people must be rooted in Jewish historical experience: since we were slaves in Egypt and have often lived as oppressed second-class citizens in ghettos, deprived of freedom and rights, we should understand the frustrations of black and brown people in America and of other minorities, here and elsewhere, their impatient yearning for equality and human dignity.

It is significant that the government of Israel has for some time been following a policy of preferential treatment for a culturally deprived minority. Special programs have been devised for the children of Oriental Jews who come from homes where there is a low level of literacy. Compensatory measures include free nurseries, longer school days and school years, special tutoring and curricula, additional funds for equipment and supplies, extra counseling services, and preferential acceptance to academic secondary schools.[17] Israel's experience with Oriental Jews might give pause to those who brag that "Jews made it on their own; why should others be given special consideration?"

Consistent with Jewish historical experience and with Jewish values related to the equality of every person, love of neighbor, treatment of strangers, and the imitation of God's attributes of justice, compassion, and kindness, it is essential that Jews work for the establishment of a society that will protect the rights of every person, entitled, as a child of God, to a life of equitable opportunities of labor, education, and human dignity.

Chapter 3

Economic Justice

Justice, justice shalt thou pursue.
—Deuteronomy 16:20

The prevalence of injustice in the world today stands in sharp contrast to Judaism's emphasis on the importance of actively seeking a just society. Note two important facts about the quotation above, which is a keynote of Jewish social values.

1. The word *justice* is repeated, a relatively infrequent occurrence in the Torah. The duplication is to bring out with the greatest possible emphasis the supreme duty of evenhanded justice to all. Bachya ben Asher commented, "Justice whether to your profit or loss, whether in word or action, whether to Jew or non-Jew."[1]
2. We are told to *pursue* justice. Hence we are not to wait for the right opportunity, the right time and place, but are to run after opportunities to practice justice.

Many other statements in the Jewish tradition show the tremendous importance placed on working for justice.

The Psalmist writes (82:3): "Give justice to the weak and the orphan; maintain the right of the afflicted and the destitute."

Isaiah (5:16) asserts:

The Lord of Hosts shall be exalted in justice,
The Holy God shows Himself holy in righteousness.

The book of Proverbs (21:3) stresses God's primary concerns:

To do righteousness and justice is preferred by God above sacrifice.

Justice is such an important concept in Judaism that, as indicated before, the patriarch Abraham even pleads with God to practice justice: "That be far from Thee to do after this manner, to slay the righteous with the wicked, . . . shall not the judge of all the earth do justly?" (Genesis 18:25)

In the Torah, justice is demanded for the slave (Exodus 21:26–27), for the stranger (Exodus 22:20), for the widow and orphan (Exodus 22:21), for women (Numbers 27:1–11), for the poor (Exodus 22:24–26), for animals (Deuteronomy 22:6–7; 25:4), and even for Israel's enemies (Deuteronomy 23:8–9).

The prophets constantly stress the importance of applying justice:

> Learn to do well—seek justice, relieve the oppressed, judge the fatherless, plead for the widow. . . . Zion shall be redeemed with justice, and her returners with righteousness.
>
> Isaiah 1:17,27

To practice justice is considered among the highest demands of prophetic religion:

> It hath been told thee, O man, what is good,
> And what the Lord doth require of thee:
> Only to do justly, love mercy,
> And walk humbly with thy God.
>
> Micah 6:8

The prophet Amos warns the people that without the practice of justice, God is repelled by their worship (5:23, 24):

> Take away from Me the noise of thy songs;
> And let Me not hear the melody of thy psalteries.
> But let justice well up as waters,
> And righteousness as a mighty stream.

The practice of justice is even part of the symbolic betrothal between the Jewish people and God:

> And I will betroth thee unto Me for ever; Yea, I will betroth thee unto Me in righteousness, justice, loving-kindness, and compassion. And I will betroth thee unto Me in faithfulness. And thou shalt know the Lord.
>
> Hosea 2:21–22

The prophets are the greatest advocates of social justice in the world's history. The prophet Jeremiah (5:28) rebukes the Jewish people when they fail to plead the cause of the orphan or help the needy. He castigates an entire generation, for "in thy shirts is found the blood of the souls of the innocent poor" (2:34). Ezekiel rebukes the entire nation for "using oppression, robbing, wronging the poor and the needy and oppressing the stranger" (22:29). Isaiah (5:8) and Micah (2:2) criticize wealthy Jews who build up large holdings of property at the expense of their neighbors. Similar statements are in Isaiah 3:13–15, Isaiah 10:1–2, and Amos 8:4–6.

Rabbi Emanuel Rackman points out that Judaism teaches a special kind of justice, an "empathic justice" that

> seeks to make people identify themselves with each other—with each other's needs, with each other's hopes and aspirations, with each other's defeats and frustrations. Because Jews have known the distress of slaves and the loneliness of strangers, we are to project ourselves into their souls and make their plight our own.[2]

Based on these teachings of the prophets and other Jewish leaders, Jews have regarded the practice of justice and the seeking of a just society as a divine imperative and an essential part of Judaism. This inspired many Jews throughout history to be leaders in struggles for better social conditions. The teachings of the Torah have been the most powerful source for justice in the world's history.

Tzedakah (Charity)

Along with its emphasis on justice, Judaism places great stress on the giving of charity. The Hebrew word for charity (tzedakah) literally means righteousness or justice. In the Jewish tradition, tzedakah is not an act of condescension from one person to another who is in need. It is the fulfillment of a mitzvah, a commandment, to a fellow human being, with equal status before God.

In the Jewish tradition, failure to give charity is equivalent to idolatry. The Talmud teaches that "tzedakah is equal to all other commandments" (Baba Bathra 9a). So important was the giving of charity by Jews that Maimonides was able to say: "Never have I seen or heard of a Jewish community that did not have a tzedakah fund."[3] He ruled that:

> He who refuses to give or gives less than he should according to his means, the court can compel him to give his share.[4]

Charity was considered so important that it took priority even over the building of the Temple. King Solomon was prohibited from using the silver and gold that David, his father, had accumulated for the building of the Temple, because that wealth should have been used to feed the poor during the three years of famine in King David's reign (1 Kings 7:51).

Judaism urges lending to needy people, to help them become economically self-sufficient:

> And if thy brother be waxen poor, and his means fail with thee; then shalt thou uphold him: . . . Take no interest of him or increase. . . . Thou shalt not give him thy money upon interest. . . .
> Leviticus 25:35–37

Every third year, the needy were to be recipients of *ma'aser* tithe (one-tenth of one's produce) (Deuteronomy 14:28; 26:12).

The general Jewish view toward aiding the poor is indicated in the following verse from the Torah:

> If there be among you a needy man, one of thy brethren, within any of thy gates, in thy land which the Lord thy God giveth thee, thou shalt not harden thy heart, nor shut thy hand from thy needy brother; but thou shalt surely open thy hand unto him, and shalt surely lend him sufficient for his need in that which he wanteth.
> Deuteronomy 15:7–8

According to Maimonides, the highest form of *tzedakah* is to prevent a person from becoming poor by providing a loan, a gift, or a job so that he can adequately support himself. Consistent with this concept is the following Talmudic teaching:

> It is better to lend to a poor person than to give him alms, and best of all is to provide him with capital for business.
> Shabbat 63a

Hence Jews should help poor people while working for a just society in which there would be no poverty. In Judaism, the idea of *tzedakah* is intertwined with the pursuit of social justice.[5]

Acts of Loving Kindness

As important as *tzedakah* (charity) is, the Jewish tradition states that even greater is *gemilut chasadim* ("acts of loving kindness"):

He who gives a coin to a poor man is rewarded with six blessings, but he who encourages him with kind words is rewarded with eleven blessings.

Baba Batra 88b

The sages interpret acts of loving kindness to mean every type of gracious action, such as hospitality to wayfarers, dowering of poor brides, visiting the sick, and comforting mourners.

Gemilut chasadim is deemed superior to acts of charity in several ways:

No gift is needed for it but the giving of oneself; it may be done to the rich as well as to the poor; and it may be done not only to the living, but also to the dead (through burial).

Mishneh Torah, Hilchot Avadim 9:8

The purpose of the entire Torah is to teach *gemilut chasadim*. The Torah starts and ends with an act of loving kindness.

For in the third chapter of Genesis, the verse reads: "The Lord God made for Adam and his wife garments of skin and clothed them." (Genesis 3:21), and the last book of Moses reports: ". . . and He buried him in the valley" (Deuteronomy 34:6).

Jewish Views on Poverty

Judaism places emphasis on justice and charity and kindness to the poor because of the great difficulties poor people face:

If all afflictions in the world were assembled on one side of the scale and poverty on the other, poverty would outweigh them all.

Exodus Rabbah, Mishpatim 31:14

Judaism believes poverty is destructive to the human personality and negatively shapes a person's life experiences.

The ruin of the poor is their poverty.

Proverbs 10:15

Where there is no sustenance, there is no learning (no Torah).

Pirke Avot 3:21

The poor man's wisdom is despised, and his words are not heard.

Ecclesiastes 9:16

Similar statements appear in Betza 32a, Eruvin 41, and Proverbs 14:20.

The negative effects of poverty are so severe that the Talmud makes the startling statement that "the poor person is considered as if he were dead" (Nedarim 64b). Judaism does not encourage an ascetic life; insufficiency of basic necessities is not considered the path toward holiness.

Many provisions of the Torah are designed to aid the poor: The corners of the field are to be left uncut for the poor to pick; the gleanings of the wheat harvest and fallen fruit are to be left for the needy; during the Sabbatical year, the land is to lie fallow so the poor may eat of whatever grows freely (Leviticus 19:10).

Failure to treat the poor properly is considered a desecration of God. "Whoso mocketh the poor blasphemeth his Maker" (Proverbs 17:5). Our father, Abraham, always went out of his way to aid the poor. He set up inns on the highways so that the poor and the wayfarer would have access to food and drink when in need.[6] Even when recovering from his circumcision, he waited in the heat of the day for needy people to pass by, so that he could show them hospitality.

There are several indications in the Jewish tradition that God sides with the poor and oppressed. He intervened in Egypt on behalf of poor, wretched slaves. His prophets constantly castigated those who oppressed the needy. Two proverbs reinforce this message. A negative formulation is in Proverbs 14:31: "He who oppresses a poor man insults his Maker." Proverbs 19:17 puts it more positively: "He who is kind to the poor lends to the Lord." Hence helping a needy person is like providing a loan to the Creator of the universe.

Compassion

Closely related to justice and charity is the importance Judaism places on compassion. The entire Torah is designed to teach us to be compassionate:

> ... The purpose of the laws of the Torah is to promote compassion, loving-kindness and peace in the world.[7]

26

The Talmud teaches that "Jews are compassionate children of compassionate parents, and one who shows no pity for fellow creatures is assuredly not of the seed of Abraham, our father" (Betzah 32b). The rabbis considered Jews to be distinguished by three characteristics: compassion, modesty, and benevolence (Yebamot 79a). As indicated previously, we are to feel empathy for strangers, "for ye were strangers in the land of Egypt" (Deuteronomy 10:19). The *bircat ha-mazon* (grace recited after meals) speaks of God feeding the whole world with compassion.

We are not only to have compassion on Jews, but on all who are in need. For:

> Have we not all one Father?
> Hath not one God created us?
>   Malachi 2:10

We are even commanded to help our enemies when they lack sufficient food or water (Proverbs 25:21).

Rabbi Samson Raphael Hirsch writes very eloquently of the importance of compassion:

> Do not suppress this compassion, this sympathy especially with the sufferings of your fellowman. It is the warning voice of duty, which points out to you your brother in every sufferer, and your own sufferings in his, and awakens the love which tells you that you belong to him and his sufferings with all the powers that you have. Do not suppress it! . . . See in it the admonition of God that you are to have no joy so long as a brother suffers by your side.[8]

Rabbi Samuel Dresner indicates "Compassion is the way God enters our life in terms of man's relation to his fellowman."[9]

The Jewish stress on compassion found expression in many groups and activities in Jewish history. There was a Bikur Cholim Society to provide medical expenses for the sick whose families had insufficient funds, and to visit the ill and bring them comfort and cheer; a Malbish Arumim Society to provide clothing for the poor; a Hachnasat Kalah Society to dower needy brides; a Bet Yetomin Society to aid orphans; a Talmud Torah Organization to support a free school for needy children; a Gemilat Chesed Society to lend money at no interest to those in need; an Ozer Dalim Society to dispense charity to the poor; a Hachnasat Orchim Society to provide shelter for homeless travelers; a Chevrah Kaddishah Society to attend to the proper burial of the dead; and Essen Tag Institution to provide food and shelter for poor students who were attending schools in the community.[10]

Judaism also stresses compassion for animals. There are many laws in the Torah based on kindness to animals. A farmer is commanded not to muzzle his ox when he threshes corn (Deuteronomy 25:4) and not to plow with an ox and an ass together (Deuteronomy 22:10), since the weaker animal would not be able to keep up with the stronger. Animals are to be allowed to rest on the Sabbath Day (Exodus 20:8–10, 23:12). A person is commanded to feed his animals before sitting down to his own meal. These concepts are summarized in the Hebrew phrase *tsa'ar ba'alei chayim*—the mandate not to cause "sorrow to any living creature."

The Psalmist indicates God's concern for animals, for "His tender mercies are over all His creatures" (Psalm 145:9). He pictures God as "satisfying the desire of every living creature (Psalm 145:16) and "providing food for the beasts and birds" (Psalm 147:9). Perhaps the Jewish attitude toward animals is epitomized by the statement in Proverbs "The righteous person regards the life of his beast" (Proverb 12:10). In Judaism, one who does not treat animals with compassion cannot be a righteous individual.[11]

Judaism and Business Ethics

The rabbis of the Talmud give concrete expression to the many prophetic teachings regarding justice and righteousness. They indicate in detail what is proper when conducting business. Rabbinic literature translates prophetic ideals into the language of the marketplace in terms of duties of employers to employees and workers to their employers, fair prices, the avoidance of false weights and measures, proper business contracts, and fair methods of competition.

Rava, a fourth-century Babylonian teacher, taught the wealthy merchants of his town the importance of scrupulous honesty in business dealings. He stated that on Judgment Day the first question God asks a person is "Were you reliable in your business dealings?" (Shabbat, 31a). The rabbis stress that a person's word is a sacred bond that should not be broken. The Mishnah states that God will exact punishment for those who do not abide by their promises (Baba Metzia 4:2). Cheating a Gentile is considered even worse than cheating a Jew, for "besides being a violation of the moral law, it brings Israel's religion into contempt, and desecrates the name of Israel's God" (Baba Kamma, 113b).

The sages are very critical of attempts to take away a person's livelihood by unfair competition (Sanhedrin 81a). Their overall view of business ethics can be summarized by the verses "And thou shalt do that which is right and good in the sight of the Lord" (Deuteronomy 6:18), and "better is a little with righteousness than great revenues with injustice" (Proverbs 16:8).

The very high ethical standards of the Talmudic sages are exemplified by the following story:

> Reb Saphra had wine to sell. A certain customer came in to buy wine at a time when Reb Saphra was saying the *Sh'ma* prayer, which cannot be interrupted by speaking. The customer said, "Will you sell me the wine for such an amount?" When Reb Saphra did not respond, the customer thought he was not satisfied with the price and raised his bid. When Reb Saphra had finished his prayer, he said, "I decided in my heart to sell the wine to you at the first price you mentioned; therefore I cannot accept your higher bid."
>
> She'iltot, Parshat VaYechi

It is essential that Jews work to establish systems and conditions consistent with the basic Jewish values discussed so far: justice, compassion, kindness, the sacredness of every life, the imitation of God's attributes, love of neighbors, consideration of the stranger, and the highest of business ethics.

Chapter 4

Economic Democracy

*The pursuit of profit has led to the condition where the great
treasures of natural resources are accumulated in the hands of
the few individuals who, because of further profits, have brought
to tens of millions of human beings pain, hunger and want. Does
this not show clearly the wickedness of the present capitalist order, which is in glaring contradiction to the religious ethical
tendencies of Judaism? . . . The fight for Socialism is the fight
for human liberation. . . . Moral rebirth and not mere economic
reconstruction. The fight for Socialism . . . must be firstly a fight
for values, higher spiritual values, infinite values.*
—Rabbi Abraham B. Bick[1]

Judaism does not recommend one type of economic system for all times
and places. However, its principles of social conduct are clear. The
Torah is opposed to all types of exploitation and to concentration of
wealth in the hands of a few, with the resultant impoverishment of
many. The Torah desires that all people should work and enjoy the
fruits of their labor.

Elements of modern capitalism are inconsistent with basic Jewish
values related to justice, compassion, concern for the poor, the dignity
of every person, and love of our fellow humans:

- While Jewish values are epitomized in the visions of prophets,
  capitalist values are often dreams of profits. Things are done in
  a capitalistic society not because they are just, righteous, or
  kind, but because they are profitable.
- While Judaism teaches "love thy neighbor as thyself," under
  capitalism the motto must be "suspect thy neighbor as thyself."
  One never knows if a person being dealt with is behaving hon-
  estly. Recent surveys have shown that many automobile me-
  chanics and other repair people act dishonestly when they think

they can get away with it. While Torah scrolls are supposed to be used to teach Jewish values, hundreds of them have recently been stolen in New York City and used as a source of unjust profit, according to the Anti-Defamation League of B'nai B'rith.

- While Judaism teaches that each person is created in God's image and hence is of infinite worth, under capitalism people are treated primarily as consumers. Advertisers do not attempt to educate people or increase their sensitivity, but rather appeal to their greed and insecurity.

- While Judaism teaches that life is sacred and we must make great efforts to save lives, under capitalism lives are often endangered to increase profits. Hence we see massive advertising of cigarettes, extensive lobbying by industry against increased job safety for workers, and corporate efforts to circumvent anti-pollution legislation.

- While Judaism stresses *tzedek, tzedek tirdof* ("justice, justice shalt thou pursue") and that God is sanctified through acts of justice, society is filled with injustice. There are great income gaps. While a small minority lead lives devoted to consumption and waste, millions of God's children lack adequate food, shelter, health care, sanitary facilities, and education.

- While Judaism mandates that we practice compassion for animals and avoid inflicting unnecessary pain, in order to maximize profits, animals are treated like machines.

- While Judaism asserts that each person is "his brother's keeper" and that "we must be kind to the stranger, for we were strangers in the land of Egypt," under capitalism each person is primarily out for himself and his family. The primary attitudes are "Lower my taxes," "Cut services for others," "Let George do it," and "Where's mine?"

- While Judaism asserts the need for a jubilee every fifty years when wealth is redistributed and property is returned to the original owner, under capitalism there are very large and increasing gaps in people's income. Due to the tremendous power that wealth provides, these gaps are likely to continue growing, making unrest and revolution more likely.

- While Judaism stresses the dignity of labor and creative work is considered necessary for every person, under our system alienated workers try to do as little work as possible for as much pay as they can get. Few people take pride in their workmanship.

- While Judaism teaches that God is the Father of all people and that one person was created to teach our common ancestry and thus there must be no prejudice against people because of race, religion, nationality, or sex, there is much discrimination in our society. Each group is pitted against other groups if it wishes to improve economically.

Can modern capitalism be reconciled with Judaism? Can a system that emphasizes the pursuit of personal financial gain without concern for the needs and welfare of others be consistent with Jewish values? Under capitalism we have what philosopher Richard Lichtman calls "the alienation of economic activity from moral concern."[1a] Can Jews accept this separation of economic and moral concerns when we affirm a Creator whose laws and concern extend to all of life?

Many of the world's people today face economic conditions similar to those indicated in the following passages from the book of Job (24:5–11):

> Lonely as wild asses in the wilderness
> They go forth to their labor;
> They must hunt the desert for sustenance,
> There is no harvest for the homeless.
> They must harvest fields that are not theirs. . . .
> Naked must they pass the night for lack of clothes.
> They have no covering from the cold.
> They are drenched by the downpour of the mountains,
> They must embrace the base rock for want of shelter.
> They must go naked, without garments;
> Hungry, they must carry the sheaves.
> Shut in by walls, they must press the oil;
> Thirsty, they must press the wine-press.

Under a profit-based system where each person seeks gain, first and foremost, the following words of Jeremiah are valid today:

> Run to and fro through the streets. . . .
> Look and take note!
> Search her squares to see
> If you can find a man,
> One who does justice
> And seeks truth; . . .
> But they all alike had broken the yoke,
> They had burst the bonds. . . .

From the least to the greatest of them,
Everyone is greedy for unjust gain;
And from prophet to priest
Everyone deals falsely. . . .
There is nothing but oppression within her.
Jeremiah 5:1,5; 6:13; 8:10; 6:6

The fact that Jewish ethical teachings are inconsistent with a
profit-based system was explicitly stated in a pronouncement of the
Rabbinical Assembly of America in 1934, in the midst of the Depression:

> In all of Jewish ethical tradition, it is assumed as axiomatic
> that men must live for each other, that mutual aid and human
> cooperation are indispensable both for peace in society and for
> moral excellence in the individual. Judaism has always asserted
> the brotherhood of man. If this concept has any meaning for life
> at all, it insists that men must live cooperatively for the common
> good.
>
> We therefore hold an individualistic, profit-inspired economy
> to be in direct conflict with the ideals of religion. We maintain
> that our present system, based, as it is, on acquisitiveness and
> selfish competition, is in practice a denial of human brotherhood.
> It exalts the aggrandizement of the individual above the interests
> of the group, it emphasizes the competitive rather than the co-
> operative elements in human character. It means that our social
> order is based on the theorem of "Every man for himself " rather
> than on the ideal of mutual aid. Our system of individualism has
> degraded human character, it has appealed to the most selfish
> instincts in men. It has been tried and found woefully wanting.
> Under the policy of laissez-faire, society has led itself to the verge
> of a complete collapse. It has created prosperity for a few and
> destitution for the multitude.
>
> We hold that only a cooperative economy, only one which has
> for its objective the enrichment of all rather than profit for a
> few—only such an economy can be moral, can elevate man and
> can function successfully. Wherefore we look to the ultimate elim-
> ination of the profit system as the basis of our national economy.
> We would have our present economy of individualism supplanted
> by one in which a socially controlled industry and agriculture
> would have for their objective not profits for a few but the fullness
> of life for all.

As will be indicated in later chapters, the practices of modern
capitalism are a prime cause of ecological damage, poverty, hunger,

resource scarcities, and war. For global survival, it is necessary that it be replaced by a more just and humane system.

The system most consistent with Jewish values is one of economic democracy: Democratic Socialism, somewhat modified in consonance with Jewish teaching. What does this mean? First, let us clearly indicate what it does not mean: It is certainly not the type of system in the Soviet Union; it is not undemocratic and certainly not oppressive; it does not involve a small elite that makes the major decisions and controls most of the wealth and power; it does not mean that you're told where to work, what to buy, where to live, what opinions to hold; it does not mean that you have no personal possessions and cannot own a home or a car.

Formulating a detailed program for Democratic Socialism is beyond the scope of this book. But some key features (all consistent with Jewish values) would include:

- high priority and value given to human life and well-being, rather than money and possessions;
- people treated as ends, not means (consistent with the concept that people are created in God's image, demonstrating respect for their dignity, ability, and potential);
- social ownership and democratic control of the major economic resources for the benefit of everyone (this does not mean that every single business would be taken over by the workers. It does mean that the important economic institutions of the country would be controlled by the people, directly or through elected representatives);
- a more equitable distribution of income, wealth, and services;
- a broader distribution of power, with people at the local level participating in decisions that affect them;
- progressive taxes designed to reduce inequality, rather than to magnify it; and
- prices and wages set at a level where every person could obtain adequate food, clothing, and shelter.

While the above changes would be extremely valuable, it is not enough merely to change the methods of production and distribution and to establish more democratic decision making. It is also essential to radically change people's outlook and behavior. This was powerfully discussed by Leib From, a Polish Poale Agudas Israel leader:

> For of what avail a change of the social order, a mechanical change of the means of production, if human beings will remain the same

sinful and egotistic individuals that they are now? We must create not only a new order, but principally a new man, a humane and just individual. For if human beings will remain evil, no change of social system will avail; evil persons will bring harm and cause suffering to their fellows in every society, for the opportunities for wrongdoing will always exist.[2]

Perhaps the closest model for economic democracy is the kibbutz, "a collective settlement in Israel, built on the principles of collective production, self-labour, communal sharing of the fruits of that labor, absence of private property, and government by democratic decisions."[3] Kibbutz members believe that they are putting Jewish teachings into practice by building a classless society where each person's abilities are used to the fullest and there is equitable distribution of what is produced. While the kibbutzim still face many problems, they have advanced considerably through collective efforts and have made major contributions to Israel's agriculture, industry, and defense.[4] By contrast, much of Israel's economy, which is based on capitalism, faces major problems today.

You may be wondering, *Why should I consider socialism? I'm doing well under capitalism. I have a good job and a home and am able to purchase what I need for my family. And I have the freedom to do what I want, work where I want, travel where I want.*

But are things all that good? Can't they be much better for you and everyone else? Are there areas near your home where you and your family are afraid to go, especially at night? Is your transportation system as good as it should be? Are you concerned about increases in air pollution, acid rain, and toxic wastes? Do you feel that our government is doing enough to make sure that the foods you eat are adequately inspected? Are you satisfied with material presented on television and in movies? Are you happy with the values our society represents today? Do you feel that you can trust people to give you a fair deal? Do you feel more secure as the arsenal of super weapons keeps growing? Do you ever consider that our well being is built upon the exploitation of other people? Do you think people can really learn ethical, religious values in a society whose mottos often are "What's in it for me?" and "Do unto others before they do unto me"?

Some people may wonder why Democratic Socialism is being considered. Isn't it a utopian dream that can never be reached, especially in the United States? Consider, however, that Theodore Herzl's statement, "If you will it, it is no dream," has been demonstrated by the establishment of the state of Israel and its survival and great progress, under unbelievable difficulties. And even if total economic democracy cannot be fully established, even a partial pursuit of this goal can produce many benefits.

Socialism in the Jewish Tradition

While the Torah does not advocate socialism, many of its teachings seem most consistent with this economic system. When the Jews wandered in the wilderness after the exodus from Egypt and in the early years in the land of Israel, the people were strongly egalitarian; there was no hierarchy of kings or rulers. Decisions were reached democratically by the assemblage of one person from each family of the tribe. There was virtually communal ownership of property, at least of wealth-producing property. The rights to pasture lands and to wells were vested in the tribe as a unit, and private property was virtually nonexistent.

The manna that nourished the Israelities in the desert teaches lessons consistent with socialism. Each day when the Israelites collected the manna, some more and some less, when they measured the quantity at home it always turned out to be one omer per person. This teaches that there is no need to gather and amass things at the expense of others.

Those who tried to save some manna in order to store it up found that it rotted and bred worms. The lesson here is that when people become greedy or spend excessive time gathering possessions, they become oblivious to the important elements in life, and that which they already have turns rotten.

The manna also teaches a lesson about the Sabbath, which can be related to socialistic values. The people were told to gather two portions on Friday: one for that day and one for the Sabbath, when they were not to go out to collect. Those who went out to gather manna on the Sabbath found there was none in the fields. Thus the Sabbath is to be a cessation from the constant amassing of wealth and possessions, a time for dedication to human values and for appreciation that God's bounties are sufficient if people live in peace and brotherhood rather than trying to get ahead of others.

The Israelites were not satisfied with their simple diet of manna. They cried out for flesh to eat. God and Moses were very angry that the people had not learned the lessons of simple, cooperative living taught by the manna and life in the wilderness. Finally, God relented and provided quails for the people to eat. But while they were chewing on the flesh, a plague broke out and many people were killed (Numbers

11:4–33). While the manna was the staple food for forty years and kept them in good health, the one time they deviated from their simple diet and lusted for more, many deaths occurred.

What about the many laws in the Torah related to private property? These no more sanction the worse aspects of corporate capitalism than the many laws in the Torah related to slaves sanction present-day slavery or the laws concerning polygamy are endorsements of that practice. God realizes that the highest ideals of the Torah cannot always be realized and hence provides laws to reduce the damage caused by acts which are permitted as concessions to people's weakness.

Significantly, division of property was initially part of the Torah's plan to insure social equality. Originally, land was distributed by Joshua among the Israelite tribes, using the principle that "To the more [larger tribe] thou shalt give the greater inheritance, and to the fewer [smaller tribe] thou shalt give the lesser inheritance" (Numbers 26:54). Hence the first distribution of land was on the basis of social need, not privilege.

To avoid conditions whereby, due to bad fortune, a family might be compelled to sell or mortgage its land and thereby suffer for generations, a complete redistribution of land every fifty years was provided for by the Jubilee law: "In the year of the jubilee, ye shall return every man unto his possession" (Leviticus 25:13). This law protecting property rights in ancient Israel was designed to insure social equality. Hence the Torah's concept of property rights was far different from that of modern capitalism, which tends to lead to great concentrations of wealth while many people suffer from poverty.

The basis for the Jubilee year, as for other legislation designed to help the unfortunate, such as the laws related to leaving the gleanings of the harvest and the corners of the field for the poor, is the principle that "the earth is the Lord's" (Psalm 24:1). In proclaiming the Jubilee year, the Torah states its reason for the periodic revolution in property rights: "For the land is mine; for ye are strangers and settlers with me" (Leviticus 25:23). As indicated before, in light of the Torah, a person's rights to property are not those of an owner, but rather of a steward as co-partner with God in preserving and protecting the earth and seeing that its resources are used for the benefit of everyone. As Rabbi Eleazer of Bertothas says, "Give unto Him of what is His, seeing that you and what you have are His" (Pirke Avot 3:8). King David expressed a similar idea: "For all things come of You and of Your own have we given You" (1 Chronicles 29:14).

Consistent with these principles, the Talmud, though recognizing property rights, did not consider such rights unbounded and limited them greatly, even eliminating them in some instances for the common good. For example, the Halacha (Jewish law) prohibits profit related to "fraudulent misrepresentation" (Baba Metzia 49b). It opposes monopolization of basic necessities by banning hoarding for the purpose of increasing prices (Baba Batra 90b). The Talmud prohibits the export of articles of food to foreign countries if this would increase the domestic price of these articles (Baba Batra 90b). For the common good, the rabbis even justify the confiscation of private property in some cases (Yebamot 89b; Gittin 36b).

While Judaism sanctions private property, it gives priority to human rights. Hence any hungry person could, without obtaining the owner's permission, help himself to the produce in a field, as long as he did not carry away food to be sold for his own profit (Deuteronomy 23:25,26). The biblical tithe was an obligatory contribution imposed on all, so that "the stranger and the fatherless and the widow shall come and eat and be satisfied" (Deuteronomy 14:29).

No person had absolute control over his own property. A person could be punished for cutting down a young tree in his own garden, because he had destroyed what ultimately belonged to God and was to be used for everyone's benefit. A person who owned a well had to make the water available for the needs of the inhabitants of nearby communities. Henry George used the biblical concept of property distribution as the basis for his "single tax system":

> Everywhere in the Mosaic institutions is the land treated as the gift of the Creator to his common creatures which no one had the right to monopolize. Everywhere it is, not your estate, or your property, not the land which you bought, or the land which you conquered but "the land which the Lord God gives you. . . ." Moses not only provided for the fair division of the land among the people, and for making it fallow and common every seventh year, but by the institution of the Jubilee, he provided for a redistribution of the land every fifty years.[5]

Consistent with the principle that "the earth is the Lord's" and that we are thus only stewards, custodians, and guardians of what land we "possess," the Talmud stresses that things that are essential to the life of the community should not be owned and controlled by any individual or group. The sages discuss a well of water that was essential to people in a village. They conclude that the title to the well should be maintained in trust by the community, so that it would be open and accessible to all, without cost.[6] Hence Judaism points to social possession and control of all social enterprises essential to life. Ideally, this means that the earth's vast resources are to be held in trust for and developed for the welfare of every person, and not for the enrichment of the few who may have control.

Reform and Conservative rabbinical groups have passed resolutions supporting this principle. In 1934, the Social Justice Commission of the Central Conference of American Rabbis (Reform) stated that for society's safety, basic social enterprises should not be left in the control of private groups, which consider private profit ahead of community service. They advocated nationalization of banking, power plants, housing, and transportation and communication systems.[7]

In the same year, the Rabbinical Assembly (of Conservative rabbis) stated that some social enterprises, such as banking and credit, power, transportation, and communication, were so essential to community welfare that they must be publicly owned.[8]

In the late 1800s and early 1900s, many Jews were actively involved in socialist movements in Europe and the U.S. in reaction to the exploitive conditions they faced. They felt that the salvation of the Jewish people could only come about as part of the salvation of humanity.[9] Morris Hillquit, a Jewish Socialist leader in New York in the early years of the twentieth century, gave a typical view:

> I am a socialist because I cannot be anything else. I cannot accept the ugly world of capitalism, with its brutal struggles and needless suffering, its archaic and irrational economic structure, its cruel social contrasts, its moral callousness and spiritual degradation.[10]

Based on such Jewish values as justice, compassion, and concern for the poor, Jews should be in the forefront of efforts to establish economic democracy, an economic system that would provide dignity and basic human necessities to every person. They should work for Democratic Socialism using methods consistent with Torah teachings: elevating individuals through religious ethical education, forming worker's cooperatives such as the Israeli kibbutzim, and striving for peaceful changes.

Chapter 5

Ecology

In the hour when the Holy one, blessed be He, created the first man,
He took him and let him pass before all the trees of the Garden of Eden and said to him:
"See my works, how fine and excellent they are!
Now all that I have created, I created for your benefit.
Think upon this and do not corrupt and destroy My world,
For if you destroy it, there is no one to restore it after you."
—Ecclesiastes Rabbah 7:28

After God created the world, "Behold, it was very good" (Genesis 1:31). The air was clean, the waters were pure, and everything was in harmony. Unfortunately, this cannot be said about the world today, with its many ecological crises:

- The earth's major ecological systems—our fishing areas, forests, croplands, and grasslands—are all endangered.[1]
- Nearly every U.S. lake and river is polluted.[2]
- The 80 billion pounds of hazardous waste produced in the U.S. each year,[3] much of it improperly disposed of, has resulted in hundreds of chemical time bombs such as those at Love Canal, near Niagara Falls, and at Times Beach, Missouri, which caused many illnesses and forced people to leave their homes.
- Acid rain has damaged 3,000 lakes and 25,000 miles of streams in the Northeastern United States. Over 200 lakes in the Adirondacks are officially dead. "Acid fog" at Corona del Mar, near Los Angeles, has been measured to be as much as 100 times as bad as acid rain.[4]
- We are rapidly running out of space in which to dump garbage. Over half of all American cities now face or will soon face problems of waste disposal. The Fresh Kills landfill on Staten Island,

the world's largest garbage dump, is a symbol of our wasteful-ness. To meet New York City's monumental garbage disposal needs, the landfill may become a 510-foot mountain of garbage. People like the convenience of our throwaway life-style, but don't want disposal units built near them.

- Agricultural methods, particularly one-crop farming and the extensive use of chemical pesticides and fertilizers, have reduced soil fertility, caused extensive erosion, and badly polluted waters with runoffs. This may sharply reduce agricultural productivity in the future.
- We have created pesticides in order to reduce crop losses to pests. But because insects build up immunities and predators are also wiped out as the pesticides move up the food chain, losses to pests are greater then ever.

   The U.S. Environmental Protection Agency (EPA) estimates that in 1946 U.S. farmers used 50 million pounds of pesticides and lost 7 percent of their crop before harvest. Thirty years later, they were using twelve times more pesticide, but were losing almost twice as much of their crop before harvest.[5] Meanwhile, dangerous pesticides have penetrated into virtually all of the world's fish and animal population.

- For many women, breast feeding may be dangerous, due to the high concentration of PCBs and other pollutants in mothers' milk.[6]
- A recent World Bank study concluded that in poor countries, such as Colombia, "large numbers of farm families . . . try to eke out an existence on too little land, often on slopes . . . [of] 45 degrees or more. As a result, they exploit the land very se-verely, adding to erosion and other (environmental) problems, and even so are not able to make a decent living."[7]

The extreme differences between conditions at the time of creation and conditions today are indicated in the following (You will recognize the first, third, fifth, and seventh paragraphs as being from Genesis.)

   In the beginning God created the heavens and the earth. The earth was without form and void, and darkness was upon the face of the deep; and the Spirit of God was moving over the face of the waters.
   In the beginning of the technological age, man recreated the heavens and the earth. To the earth he gave new form with dynamite and bulldozer, and the void of the heavens he filled with smog.

And God said, "Let there be a firmament in the midst of the waters. . . . Let the waters under the heavens be gathered into one place, and let the dry land appear."

Then man took oil from beneath the ground and spread it over the waters, until it coated the beaches with slime. He washed the topsoil from the fertile prairies and sank it in the ocean depths. He took waste from his mines and filled in the valleys, while real estate developers leveled the hills. And man said, "Well, business is business."

Then God said, "Let the earth put forth vegetation, plants yielding seed and fruit trees bearing fruit in which is their seed, each according to its kind, upon the earth. . . . Let the earth bring forth living creatures according to their kinds." And it was so. And God saw that it was good.

But man was not so sure. He found that mosquitos annoyed him, so he killed them with DDT. And the robins died, too, and man said, "What a pity." Man defoliated forests in the name of modern warfare. He filled the streams with industrial waste—and his children read about fish . . . in the history books.

So God created man in his own image; in the image of God He created him. And God blessed them, and God said to them, "Be fruitful and multiply, and fill the earth and subdue it, and have dominion over . . . every living thing."

So man multiplied—and multiplied—and spread his works across the land until the last green glade was black with asphalt, until the skies were ashen and the waters reeked, 'til neither bird sang nor child ran laughing through cool grass. So man subdued the earth and made it over in his image, and in the name of progress he drained it of its life. . . .
. . . Until the earth was without form and void, and darkness was once again upon the face of the deep, and man himself was but a painful memory in the mind of God.[8]

Unfortunately, the outlook for the future is even bleaker. According to "The Global 2000 Report to the President,"[9]

If present trends continue, the world in 2000 will be more crowded, more polluted, less stable ecologically, and more vulnerable to disruption than the world we live in now. Serious stresses involving population, resources, and environment are clearly visible ahead. . . . Regional water shortages will become more severe. . . . Significant losses of world forests will continue. . . . Serious deterioration of agricultural soils will occur worldwide, due to erosion, loss of organic matter, desertification, salinization, . . . Acid rain from increased consumption of fossil fuels (especially coal) threatens damage to lakes, soils, and crops. . . . Indeed, the problems of preserving the carrying capacity of the earth and sustaining the possibility of a decent life for the human beings that inhabit it are enormous and close upon us. . . .

It has been estimated that there could be a loss of a million present species by the end of the century due to destruction of forests and other natural habitats, primarily in underdeveloped nations. This loss of genetic diversity could have severe ecological consequences.[10]

Jacques Cousteau, Jacques Picard, and other oceanographers have predicted that the oceans could be dead by the year 2000, due to the tremendous amounts of pollutants that are discarded in them.[11]

Environmental Problems in Israel Today

Israel's environment has been badly damaged recently. This has resulted from a combination of quickly growing population, rapid industrialization and mechanization of agriculture, extensive urbanization, and insufficient environmental concern due to many other pressing problems related to survival and the need to absorb many immigrants quickly.

Israel's environmental problems were extensively reviewed in an article by Rochelle Saidel Wolk in the November/December 1980 edition of *Women's American ORT Reporter*, titled "Israel's Other Enemies." She points out that, unless action is taken soon, Israel's environmental problems may eventually dwarf her security and economic difficulties.

The severe ecological problems that face Israel include the following:

- Lake Kinneret is endangered due to the raising of the sea level caused by the draining of the Huleh valley, the constant decrease in the water level, and water pollution.[12]
- In some urban areas, streets, parks, and neighborhoods are neglected and unkempt and sometimes completely dilapidated. Many people have ceased walking for enjoyment in some places.[13]

- Increasing noise is causing disturbances in human organic systems. Causes include heavy motor traffic, increasing industrialization, lack of adequate insulation, frequent nonobservance of rules, and rapidly increasing air traffic.[14]
- Haifa's air quality is threatened by the Haifa oil refineries. Irregularities in burning create sooty and carcinogenic smoke.[15]
- The most polluted river in Israel is the Kishon, which flows through Haifa. After years of absorbing effluents from chemical plants and the Haifa oil refineries, parts of the river look solid rather than liquid. Although there is currently a five-year plan to clean up the river, industries still have not been forced to comply with environmental standards, and cleaning a river can take generations.[16]

While the threat of environmental pollution is seldom raised, the absence of pure air and water could make Israel's other worries merely academic. The country has been accumulating many serious environmental hazards. Jack D. Lauber, a professional engineer who is chief of the Toxic Materials Section of the New York State Department of Environmental Conservation, recently visited Israel as an air-pollution consultant to the Ministry of Interior. In a letter printed in the December 12, 1979 *Jerusalem Post,* he described Israeli environmental problems:

> I've seen once-beautiful streams that are now foul open sewers, and improperly disposed toxic wastes that pollute Israel's waters, land and air, as well as tons of common refuse which make a once-beautiful land a junkyard.[17]

Lauber warned that, while Israel's pollution may not soon result in deaths, the rapid increase in toxic chemical wastes can result in time bombs for future generations. He stated that Israel's environmental programs lag about fifteen years behind those of Western Europe and the U.S., but "environmental protection is not a luxury that Israel can afford later, but is a necessity now."[18]

Jewish Values Related to Ecology

Judaism has always been extremely concerned about environmental protection. This is based on the fundamental concepts that "the earth is the Lord's and the fullness thereof " (Psalm 24:1) and that people's role is to enhance and improve the world as "co-partners of God in the work of creation" (Shabbat 10a, 119: Sanhedrin 7).

Judaism considers God as the ultimate owner of the entire world and its resources. All the material possessions a person accumulates are really God's. Even the creativity that enables people to shape nature for greater usefulness comes from the Creator of the world.

There is an apparent contradiction between two verses in Psalms: (1) "The earth is the Lord's" (Psalm 24:1) and (2) "The heavens are the heavens of God, but the earth He has given to human beings" (Psalm 115:16). The apparent discrepancy is cleared up in the following way: Before a person says a *b'racha* (a blessing), before he acknowledges God's ownership of the land and its products, then "the earth is the Lord's"; after a person has said a *b'racha,* acknowledging God's ownership and our obligation to be stewards to see that God's works are properly used and shared, *then* "the earth He has given to human beings" (Berachot 30:5).

The Psalmist also expresses the idea that God the Creator treats every person as a partner in the work of creation (Psalm 8:4–7):

> When I look at Your heavens, the work of Your hands,
> The moon and work which you have established,
> What is man that You are mindful of him, and the son of man
>   that You do care for him?
> Yet you have made him little less than God, and do crown him
>   with glory and honor.
> You have given him dominion over the works of Your hands;
>   You have put all things under his feet. . . .

The concept that people have custodial care of the earth, as opposed to ownership, is illustrated by this story from the Talmud:

> Two men were fighting over a piece of land. Each claimed ownership and bolstered his claim with apparent proof. To resolve their differences, they agreed to put the case before the rabbi. The rabbi listened but could not come to a decision because both seemed to be right. Finally he said, "Since I cannot decide to whom this land belongs, let us ask the land." He put his ear to the ground and, after a moment, straightened up. "Gentlemen, the land says it belongs to neither of you—but that you belong to it."[19]

The produce of the field does not belong solely to the person who farms the land. The poor are entitled to a portion. Hence the Torah commanded that farmers leave the corners of their fields and the gleanings of the harvests for the poor and the stranger (Leviticus 19:9,10). These portions were not voluntary contributions based on kindness. They were, in essence, a regular divine assessment. Since God was the real owner of the land, He claimed a share of His gifts for the poor.

As a reminder that "the earth is the Lord's," land must be permitted to lie fallow every seven years (the Sabbatical year), so that "the poor of thy people may eat" (Exodus 23:10,11). The Sabbatical year also has ecological benefits; the land is given a chance to rest and renew its fertility.[20]

Since "the earth is the Lord's," property is a sacred trust given by God that must be used to fulfill His purposes. No person has exclusive control over possessions. Hence one must not waste or unnecessarily destroy anything of value. This commandment, called *bal tashchit* ("thou shalt not destroy"), is based on the following Torah statement.

> When thou shalt besiege a city a long time, in making war against it to take it, thou shalt not destroy [*bal tashchit*] the trees thereof by wielding an ax against them; for thou mayest eat of them but thou shalt not cut them down; for is the tree of the field man, that it should be besieged of thee? Only the trees of which thou knoweth that they are not trees for food, them thou mayest destroy and cut down, that thou mayest build bulwarks against the city that maketh war with thee, until it fall.
>
> Deuteronomy 20: 19–20

This prohibition against destroying fruit-bearing trees in time of warfare was extended by the Jewish sages. It is forbidden to cut down even a barren tree or to waste anything if no useful purpose is accomplished (Sefer HaChinuch, 529). The sages of the Talmud made a general prohibition against waste: "Whoever breaks vessels or tears garments, or destroys a building, or clogs up a fountain, or destroys food, violates the prohibition of *bal tashchit*" (Mishneh Torah Hilchot Melachim 6:10). *Bal tashchit* prohibits the destruction, complete or incomplete, direct or indirect, of all objects of potential benefit to people.

The seriousness with which the rabbis considered the violation of *bal tashchit* is illustrated by the following Talmudical statements:

- The sage Rabbi Hanina attributed the early death of his son to the fact that the boy had chopped down a fig tree (Baba Kamma 91b).
- Jews should be taught when very young that it is a sin to waste even small amounts of food (Berachot 52b).

● Rav Zutra taught: "One who covers an oil lamp or uncovers a naptha lamp transgresses the prohibition of *bal tashchit*" (Shabbat 67b). Each action mentioned would cause a faster (hence wasteful) consumption of the fuel.

All that God has created is meant for human welfare and sustenance. Therefore to waste and destroy is to sin against God as well as against one's fellow human beings.

The significance of *bal tashchit* has been explained as follows:

> The purpose of a mitzvah, as is well known, is to train our souls to love the good and that which is creative and useful and to refrain from all that which is destructive. The way of the righteous and men of good deeds is to love peace and take pleasure in the welfare of their fellow-man and draw them closer to the Torah. They would not wantonly destroy even a mustard seed. They are grieved and oppressed at the sight of waste and destruction. If they could save anything from being destroyed they would do so with all their power. The wicked are not so. They are the brethren of all despoilers. They are happy in destroying the world as they are in destroying themselves. . . . Generally speaking the Rabbis forbade all destructive acts and they linked one who destroys anything in anger to one who worships idols.
>
> Sefer HaChinuch 529

Rabbi Samson Raphael Hirsch stated that *bal tashchit* is the first and most general call of God: We are to "regard things as God's property and use them with a sense of responsibility for wise human purposes. Destroy nothing! Waste nothing!"[21] He defined destruction as using more things (or using things of greater value) than is necessary to attain one's aim.[22]

Judaism asserts that there is one God who created the entire earth as a unity, in ecological balance, and that everything is connected to everything else. This idea is perhaps best expressed by Psalm 104:

> . . . Thou [God] art the One Who sends forth springs into brooks,
>   that they may run between mountains,
> To give drink to every beast of the fields; the creatures of the
>   forest quench their thirst.
> Beside them dwell the fowl of the heavens; . . .
> Thou art He Who waters the mountains from His upper
>   chambers; . . .
> Thou art He Who causes the grass to spring up for the cattle
>   and herb, for the service of man, to bring forth bread from
>   the earth. . . .

How manifold art Thy works, O Lord! In wisdom hast Thou
made them all; the earth is full of Thy property. . . .

Ecology in Jewish History and Prayers

Much of early Jewish history is closely related to the natural environment. The patriarchs and their descendants were shepherds.
Their work led them into many types of natural settings, including
mountains, prairies, wilderness, and desert. They thus developed a
love and appreciation of natural wonders and beauty. According to
Charles W. Eliot, "no race has ever surpassed the Jewish descriptions
of either the beauties or the terrors of the nature which environs
man."[23]

The greatest prophet, Moses, while a shepherd, learned many facts
about nature which were useful in leading the Israelites in the desert.
The Ten Commandments and the Torah were revealed to the Jews at
Mount Sinai, in a natural setting. The forty years of wandering in the
wilderness trained Israel in the appreciation of natural beauty.

Jews have often pictured God through His handiwork in nature.
Abraham, the father of the Jewish people, when marveling at the
heavenly bodies, intuited that there must be a creator of these wonders.
The prophet Isaiah stated:

> Lift up thine eyes on high,
> And see: Who hath created these?
> He that bringeth out their host by numbers,
> He calleth them all by name;
> By the greatness of His might, for He is strong in power,
> Not one faileth.
>
> Isaiah 40:26

Many Jewish prayers extol God for His wondrous creations. In the
morning, religious Jews say the following prayer to thank God for the
new day:

> Blessed art Thou, O Lord our God, King of the universe.
> Who formest light and createst darkness,
> Who makest peace and createst all things.
> Who in mercy givest light to the earth
> And to them that dwell thereon,
> And in Thy goodness renewest the creation
> Every day continually.

How manifold are Thy works, O Lord!
In wisdom hast Thou made them all;
The earth is full of Thy possessions. . . .
Be Thou blessed, O Lord our God,
For the excellency of Thy handiwork,
And for the bright luminaries
Which Thou hast made:
They shall glorify Thee forever.

At the morning Sabbath services, the following prayer is recited: "The heavens declare the glory of God, and the firmament showeth His handiwork" (Psalms 19:2).

The sensitivity of the Torah to environmental cleanliness is illustrated by the following law, which commands disposal of sewage, even in wartime, by burial in the ground, not by dumping into rivers or littering the countryside.

> Thou shalt have a place outside the military camp, whither thou shalt go forth abroad. And thou shalt have a spade among thy weapons; and it shalt be when thou sittest down outside, thou shalt dig therewith, and shalt turn back and cover that which cometh from thee.
>
> Deuteronomy 23:13–15

The preservation of the land of Israel has been a central theme in Judaism. The three festivals (Pesach, Shavuot, and Sukkot) are agricultural as well as spiritual celebrations. Jews have prayed for dew and rain in their proper time so that there would be abundant harvests in Israel. There has traditionally been an attitude of sanctity and reverence that would militate against abuse of natural resources and the environment.

The Talmudic sages had great concern about preserving the environment and preventing pollution. They stated: "It is forbidden to live in a town which has no garden or greenery" [Kiddushin 4:12]. Threshing floors had to be placed far enough from a town so that it would not be dirtied by chaff carried by winds (Baba Batra 2:8). Tanneries had to be kept at least fifty cubits from a town and could be placed only on the east side of a town, so that odors would not be carried by the prevailing winds from the west (Baba Batra 2:8,9). The rabbis indicated a sense of sanctity toward the environment as well as the holiness of the land when they said, "The climate of the land of Israel makes one wise" (Baba Batra 1:58b).

This traditional Jewish respect for environmental quality was exhibited by Jewish pioneers in modern Israel, who drained swamps, restored forests, and reclaimed deserts.

Causes of Current Ecological Problems

The root cause of current ecological crises is that the values of our economic and production systems are completely contrary to Torah values:

- While Judaism stresses that "the earth is the Lord's" and that we are to be partners in protecting the environment, corporations consider the earth in terms of how it can be used to maximize profits, with only minor regard for negative environmental effects.

  Instead of starting with protection of the earth as a prime value and building production and economic systems consistent with this value, our production is based on the idea of maximum gain, regardless of negative ecological consequences. American corporations and utility companies make choices with maximum profit as their overriding concern. It is their misuse of technology that is at the root of the ecological crisis.[24]

- While Judaism mandates *bal tashchit,* our economy is based on waste, on buying, using, and disposing, and on planned obsolescence. Advertising constantly tries to make people feel guilty if they don't have the newest gadgets and the latest styles. Every national holiday has become an orgy of consumption with department-store sales filling parking lots with cars.

  The United States has become a throwaway society. Almost all of our beverage containers are disposables. We're using increasing numbers of plastic containers, although they harm the environment more than glass or metal containers. For convenience, we are using greater amounts of paper products each year. Many potentially valuable products that could be used for fertilizer are discarded; these include sewage sludge, garbage, agricultural and forest residues, and animal manure.

  The United States is the most wasteful country in the world. Although we have only about 5 percent of the world's people, we use about a third of the world's resources; if only 10 percent of the rest of the world used as many resources per person as we do, there would be nothing left for anybody else in the world. While consuming these resources, we cause about half the world's pollution.

Due to waste, it has been estimated that our impact on the earth's life support systems, in terms of pollution and resource consumption per person, is about fifty times that of a person in India or another undeveloped country.[25] Using this figure, our population has an impact equal to that of 11 billion Third World people, over twice the population of the world today.

Wastefulness is leading to an increasingly dangerous world. As we continue to squander energy and resources, there will be increasing demand for such things as liquefied natural gas storage tanks, nuclear power plants, off-shore drilling for oil, and coal-burning power plants. These will subject us to dangers from explosions, seepage of radioactive materials, weapons proliferation from plutonium produced by nuclear power plants, offshore oil spills, and possible climate changes.

• While Judaism teaches about a Sabbatical year in which the land will lie fallow and recover its fertility and farmers may rest, learn, and restore their spiritual values, today, under economic pressure to constantly produce more, farmers plant single crops and use excessive amounts of chemical pesticides and fertilizer, thereby reducing soil fertility and badly polluting air and water.

Jewish Values Can Help Solve the Environmental Crisis

Based on biblical values of "The earth is the Lord's" and *bal tashchit,* Jews and others who take religious values seriously must lead efforts to preserve the environment. We must work to change a competitive system that is based primarily on greed and maximization of profits and appeals to people to amass material goods, while great ecological damage occurs. We must work for an economic system that puts primary emphasis on protection of our vital ecosystems.

To reduce potential threats to the U.S. and the world, we must change to simpler, saner life-styles. Churches and synagogues, schools, and private and governmental organizations must all play a role. We must move away from wasteful jobs to jobs in such environmentally helpful areas as recycling, solar energy, and mass transit. We must design products for long lives and ease of repair. We must revise our agricultural and industrial methods so that they are less wasteful of resources and energy. There should be a presidential commission and governmental officials appointed solely to concern themselves with how we can stop being such a wasteful society

51

Changing will not be easy. since our whole society and economy are based on consumption and convenience, using and discarding. But it is essential that we make supreme efforts. Nothing less than human survival is at stake.

The proper application of Sabbath values would help end environmental pollution. The Sabbath teaches that we should not be constantly involved in exploiting the world's resources and amassing more and more possessions. On that day we are to realize our dependence on God and our responsibility to treat the earth with care and respect. This is powerfully expressed by Rabbi Samson Raphael Hirsch:

> To really observe the Sabbath in our day and age! To cease for a whole day from all business, from all work, amidst the frenzied hurry-scurry of our age! To close the stock exchanges, the stores, the factories—how would it be possible? The pulse of life would stop beating and the world perish!
> The world perish? On the contrary; it would be saved. . . .[26]

The philosophy of the Sabbatical year is another approach to environmental problems. There could be great benefits if land, on a rotational basis, could be left fallow, free from the tremendous amounts of chemicals and fertilizer that pollute air and water and reduce soil fertility. If people could get away for a (Sabbatical) year from their harried lives, from the shrieking of the marketplace, and from the constant pressure to produce and buy goods, they would have the opportunity to use their time for mental and spiritual development and perhaps to study methods of reducing pollution and other current problems.

As co-workers with God, charged with the task of being a light unto the nations and of *tikun olam* (restoring and redeeming the earth), it is essential that Jews take an active role in struggles to end pollution and waste of natural resources. Jews must work with others for radical changes in our economic and production systems, our values, and our life-styles, based on the important biblical mandate to work with God in preserving the earth.

Chapter 6

Hunger

If one takes seriously the moral, spiritual, and humanitarian values of Biblical, Prophetic, and Rabbinic Judaism, the inescapable issue of conscience that must be faced is: How can anyone justify not becoming involved in trying to help save the lives of starving millions of human beings throughout the world—whose plight constitutes the most agonizing moral and humanitarian problem in the latter half of the twentieth century?
—Rabbi Marc H. Tanenbaum

Food, its production and distribution, will be the overriding social, political, economic, environmental, and moral issue of our next decade.[1]

World hunger statistics are staggering: Over 1 billion people, nearly a quarter of the world's population, are chronically undernourished.[1a] Between 700 and 800 million people lack sufficient income to obtain the basic necessities of life.[2] Fifteen to twenty million people die annually due to hunger and its effects, including diseases brought on by lowered resistance due to malnutrition.[3]

Children are particularly hard hit by malnutrition. Three out of four whose deaths are related to hunger are children. In poor countries, over 40 percent of all deaths occur among children under five years old.[4] Ten percent of the world's children die before their first birthday.[5] At least 100,000 children annually go blind due to vitamin A deficiency in their diet. Malnourishment also brings listlessness and reduced capacity for learning and activities, which continues the legacy of poverty.

These startling statistics may make us forget the effects of hunger on one individual:

Hunger feels like pincers,
like the bite of crabs,

it burns, burns, and has no fire.
Hunger is a cold fire. . . .

For now I ask no more
than the justice of eating.[6]

The extensive hunger and malnutrition in so many parts of the world make rebellion and violence more likely. Professor Georg Borgstrom, internationally known expert on food science, fears that "the rich world is on a direct collision course with the poor of the world. . . . We cannot survive behind our Maginot line of missiles and bombs."[7] Hence the outlook for global stability is very poor, unless the problem of global hunger is soon solved. Professor Robert Heilbroner, the noted economist, predicted that in times of severe famine, countries like India will be sorely tempted to try nuclear blackmail.[8]

Jewish Teachings Related to Hunger

On Yom Kippur, the holiest day of the Jewish calendar, Jews are told, through the words of the prophet Isaiah, that their fasting and prayers are not sufficient; they must work to end oppression and provide food for the needy:

> Is not this the fast that I have chosen? To loose the chains of wickedness, to undo the bonds of oppression, and to let the oppressed go free. . . . Is it not to share thy bread with the hungry. . . ?
>
> Isaiah 58:6,7

Helping hungry people is fundamental in Judaism. The Talmud states: "Aiding the poor and hungry weighs as heavily as all the other commandments of the Torah combined" (Baba Batra 9a).

The Midrash teaches:

> God says to Israel, "My children, whenever you give sustenance to the poor, I impute it to you as though you gave sustenance to Me. . . ." Does then God eat and drink? No, but whenever you give food to the poor, God accounts it to you as if you gave food to Him.
>
> Midrash Tannaim

On Passover, we are reminded to help the needy. Besides providing *ma'ot chittim* (funds for purchasing matza) for the poor before Passover, at the Seders, we reach out to those who are hungry and in need:

> This is the bread of affliction which our ancestors ate in the
> land of Egypt.
> Let all who are hungry come and eat,
> Let all who are in need come and celebrate the Passover.

We are even admonished to feed our enemies, if they are in need:

> If your enemy is hungry, give him bread to eat.
> If your enemy is thirsty, give him water to drink.
> Proverbs 25:21

Just having compassion for the poor and hungry is not enough. A fundamental Jewish principle is that those who have much should share with less fortunate people. The Talmudic sage Hillel stresses that we must not be concerned only with our own welfare:

> If I am not for myself, who will be for me?
> But if I am for myself alone, what am I?
> Pirke Avot 1:14

The act of prolonging one's meal (on the chance that a poor person may come) so that one may share one's food is so meritorious that the table of the person who does this is particularly compared to the altar of the holy Temple (Berachot 55a).

The great importance that Judaism places on sharing is also illustrated in the following Chassidic tale:

> The story is told of a great rabbi who was given the privilege of seeing the realms of Heaven and Hell before his death. He was taken first to Hell, where he was confronted with a huge banquet room in the middle of which was a large elegant table covered with a magnificent white tablecloth, the finest china, silver, and crystal. The table was covered from one end to the other with the most delicious foods that the eyes have ever seen or the mouth tasted. And all around the table people were sitting looking at the food . . . and wailing. It was such a wail that the rabbi had never heard such a sad sound in his entire life and he thought, "With a luxurious table and the most delicious food, why do these people wail so bitterly?" As he entered the room he saw the reason for their distress. For although each was confronted with this

incredible sight before him, no one was able to eat the food. Each person's arms were splinted so that the elbows could not bend. They could touch the food but could not eat it. The anguish this caused was the reason for the great sorrow and despair.

He was next shown Heaven, and to his surprise he was confronted by the identical scene witnessed in Hell. (The large banquet room, the elegant table, the lavish settings and the sumptuous foods. And in addition, once again everyone's arms were splinted so the elbows could not bend.) Here however, there was no wailing, but rather joy greater than he had every experienced in his life. For whereas here too the people could not put the food into their *own* mouths, each picked up the food and fed it to *another*. They were thus able to enjoy not only the beautiful scene, the wonderful smells, and the delicious foods, but the joy of sharing and helping one another.[9]

Rabbi Yaakov Marcus of the Young Israel of Staten Island commented on the fact that *karpas* (eating of greens) and *yahatz* (breaking of the middle matza for later use as dessert) are next to each other in the Passover Seder service that only those who can live on simple things like greens (vegetables, et cetera) will be able to divide their possessions and share with others.[10]

To help share God's abundant harvests with the poor, Jewish farmers were instructed:

1. If less than three ears of corn were dropped during the harvest, they were not to be gleaned, but were to be left for the poor (*Leket*).

2. A sheaf forgotten by the farmer could not be retrieved but had to be left for the poor (*Shikh'hah*).

3. A corner of the field always had to be left unharvested; it was the property of the poor (Pe'ah).

4. Every third year a part of the tithe of the harvest had to be set aside for the poor (*Ma'aser Ani*).

5. On the eve of every holy day, "*mat'not Yad*," a special gift to the poor, had to be put aside.

The importance of sharing in helping others was beautifully expressed by the Holocaust victim Anne Frank, in an essay called "Give," which she wrote in March 1944:

How lovely to think that no one need wait a moment; We can start now, start slowly changing the world! How lovely that everyone, great and small, can make their contribution toward introducing justice straightaway!

Give of yourself, give as much as you can! And you can always, always give something even if it is only kindness! Give, give again and again, don't lose courage, keep it up and go on giving! No one has ever become poor from giving.

There is plenty of room for everyone in the world, enough money, riches, and beauty for all to share! God has made enough for everyone! Let us all begin then by sharing it fairly.[11]

It is fundamental Jewish belief that God provides enough for everyone's needs. In our daily prayers, it is said: "He openeth up his hand and provided sustenance to all living things" (Psalms 145:16). Jews are obligated to give thanks to God for providing enough food for themselves and all of humanity. In the *bircat ha-mazon* (grace after meals), we praise God "Who feedest the whole world with goodness, grace, loving kindness and tender mercy." The blessing is, of course, correct. God *has* provided enough for all. The bounties of nature, fairly distributed and properly consumed, would sustain all people.

Non-Causes of Hunger

There are many misconceptions about the causes of global hunger. Hunger is not caused by overpopulation, bad weather, lack of technology, or ignorance of people in poor countries.[12] These can all worsen the problem, but they do not cause it.

Population has been growing explosively in recent years. It took all of history until 1850 for the world's population to reach 1 billion people. Now the population is over 4.5 billion and is increasing by a billion people every ten to thirteen years.[13]

Yet population is not a root cause of world hunger. Africa is relatively sparsely populated and yet has much hunger. Many European countries, such as Belgium and Holland, are very densely populated but have virtually no hungry people.

Rather than being a cause of hunger, rapid population growth is more often a result of hunger. When many babies die from malnutrition and disease, couples will have many children so that some will survive. In societies where there is no unemployment insurance, Social Security, or pension programs, children, especially males, provide the only assurance that there will be help when the parents become disabled or too old to work.

In these very poor, hungry countries, the cost of raising a child is very low but the economic value in terms of the child providing assistance is great. Given these conditions, the answer to the population problem is not only in better birth control techniques, but in an improvement of the people's economic and social conditions.

Hunger is not a result of bad weather. No matter how bad the weather, the wealthy in any country always manage to eat well. In a book published in 1928, it was reported that China had a famine in some provinces every year for over 1,000 years. Today China has an agricultural system that is much less vulnerable to weather changes. They have utilized their massive labor power to sink hundreds of wells, build reservoirs, and dam rivers to insure an adequate supply of water.[14] Famine is caused by social conditions, not nature.

What about lack of technology as a cause of global hunger? In many cases, new technology has made the situation worse, since it has not been combined with necessary social and economic changes.

New "miracle" seeds (the green revolution) were proposed as an answer to inadequate food production. But these seeds require good land, proper irrigation, and heavy doses of fertilizer and pesticides. Only wealthy farmers with large farms can afford these inputs. Their increased production lowered the price of food and drove many small farmers who couldn't compete off the land.

The use of mechanization, such as on American farms, can also have negative effects. It forces many farm workers off the farms into the increasingly crowded cities, seeking employment, which often is not available. In northeast Mexico, twenty years ago the average farm acreage was four hundred acres. Now, after extensive use of technology—new seeds, machines, irrigation, fertilizer, and pesticides—the average is 2,000 acres and many small farmers have moved to the overcrowded cities.[15]

In the United States, tax-funded research in California resulted in tomato harvests so big that only a few farmers had the land and capital to take advantage of them. The result: While large operators cut costs and prospered, in only eight years, 85 percent of California's tomato growers were driven out of business.[16]

Increased production due to improved technology seldom goes to hungry people. It generally goes to wealthier people for luxury food products, to feed livestock, or for exports to more affluent countries.

The key question with regard to technology is: Who stands to gain? If technology is used to benefit small local elites while driving many people off farms, it worsens the hunger situation. If it is used cooperatively, in conjunction with a country's vast labor power and local planning and initiative so that individual peasants benefit directly from their added productivity, it can be of great value.

Is the ignorance of small farmers in poor countries a major cause of widespread hunger? On the contrary, small peasant farmers get much out of land. They work their very limited resource to the fullest because it is all they have for survival.

The problem of the poor is not due to backwardness of peasant farmers. They just have very little to work with, since ownership of land and wealth is concentrated in very few hands.

Causes of Hunger

Injustice

What, then, are the root causes of global hunger? Once again, they are related to a system of production and distribution based on inequality, injustice, and greed, which is at sharp variance with biblical values. In a policy statement on October 11, 1975, The National Council of Churches stated that the fundamental cause of world hunger was "the sinful behavior of humankind, including the denial of human solidarity; greed; and selfishness with which neighbor exploits neighbor." They further stated: "Institutionalized injustice explains more than all other factors combined why half a billion persons suffer from chronic hunger in a world which could have enough food to go around."

There is great poverty and hunger in underdeveloped countries because the social and economic inequalities prevalent in these countries prevent people from making an adequate living. Land and wealth are concentrated among a few, and with land and wealth goes power to control the destiny of the masses.

Control of land (and the things needed to make land produce)—seeds, tools, machinery, fertilizer, pesticides, and irrigation systems—is in relatively few hands:

- A UN study showed that in eighty-three Third World countries, about 3 percent of landholders controlled almost 80 percent of the land.[17] Even in the U.S., less than 6 percent of all farm owners control over half the nation's farmland.[18]
- In the U.S. and Canada, two giants, John Deere and International Harvester, control half of the tractor sales and two-thirds of the sales of combines.[19]
- There is unequal control over credit, which is needed to purchase farm equipment. In most Third World countries, farmers are forced to borrow from a big landowner or a local moneylender, often at annual interest rates as high as 200 percent.[20]

59

- There is also tightening control over the processing and marketing of food. In the U.S., of the 30,000 food processing and marketing corporations, the top 50 capture over 90 percent of the industry's profits.[21]
- Worldwide, a few corporations control the international sales of many resources. For example, only five corporations control 90 percent of all international grain shipments.[22] Hence fewer and fewer people are making decisions on how resources are used and for whose benefit.

Colonialism changed patterns of food production in many countries. The English political economist John Stuart Mill stated that colonies should not be thought of as countries at all, but as "agricultural establishments" whose sole purpose was to supply the "large community to which they belong."[23]

Using raw force and high taxes, Europeans changed the diversified agriculture of their colonies to single cash crops, often at the exclusion of staple foods. The best land was taken over to produce tea, coffee, bananas, and other crops that could be exported to enrich foreigners and local elites, at the expense of the native population. This process sowed the seeds of famine.

While the colonial period is generally over, its remnants exist in the form of neocolonialism. Underdeveloped countries must still produce cash crops in order to meet their debts and to obtain badly needed cash.[24]

In Central American and the Caribbean countries, where 80 percent of the children are undernourished, almost half the cultivated land, the best half, is used to produce five commodities for export: bananas, sugar, coffee, cocoa, and beef.[25] In the late 1960s and early 1970s, while famine worsened in the African Sahel, exports of peanuts, cotton, vegetables, and meat actually increased.[26] Thirty-six of the world's forty poorest countries export food to North America.

Underdeveloped countries are on a treadmill. They must work harder and harder just to keep up. They are prevented from developing their own resources for their own use, and conditions of trade are against them. Three tons of bananas could buy a tractor in 1960; by 1970, an equivalent tractor cost eleven tons of bananas.[27]

Multinational Corporations

Another prime condition behind the world food crisis has been the actions of multinational corporations. To maximize profits, they have brought extensive technology to poor countries, often worsening the problems of unemployment, poverty, and, ultimately, malnutrition. They have furthered the cash-crop system, buying up much valuable land for these crops at the expense of more nutritious foods for local populations. Finally, through the use of advertising and television, they have drastically changed the culture, values, and eating habits of local people.

Only three giant corporations control the $2 billion banana industry. The giant multinational corporations take most of the profits in this cash crop. Out of every final retail dollar spent on bananas, the producing country gets only about eleven cents.[28]

Under control of large corporations, much of the world's farmland is not being used to raise crops. Only about 44 percent of the world's cultivatable land is being used to grow food.[29] In Ecuador, where there is much malnutrition, just 14 percent of potential cropland is being cultivated.[30] In northeast Brazil, where most people go hungry, the large estates controlling most of the best farmland cultivate only 15 percent.

Large corporations have also often had negative effects in the United States. While farms grow larger and more mechanized, over the last twenty-five years, the number of U.S. farms has decreased by an average of over 1,900 per week.[31] Meanwhile the quality and nutritional value of the average American diet has been reduced.

Wastefulness

Still another factor that greatly worsens the global food situation is the wastefulness of affluent countries, such as the United States. Our diet is extremely wasteful. We consume about five times as much grain per person as the poorer countries; most of the grain we use is in the form of meat.[32]

It takes about eight pounds of grain to produce one pound of edible beef in a feedlot. Half of U.S. farm acreage is used to produce feed crops for livestock. Our meat-centered diet requires about seventeen times the land area per person than would be required for a purely vegetarian diet. Our agricultural system also requires tremendous inputs of chemical fertilizer and pesticides, irrigation water, and fuel, commodities becoming very scarce worldwide.

Not only is much land and resources used in the U.S. to raise beef, but the United States is the world's largest importer of beef![33] We import approximately 1 million cattle every year from Mexico, half as much beef as all Mexicans have left for themselves.[34] In spite of widespread poverty and malnutrition in Honduras, they export large amounts of beef to the U.S. Beef for export in Honduras is grown by a tiny wealthy elite (0.3 percent of the total population) who own over 25 percent of all cultivatable land.[35]

Research at the Institute for Food and Development in California has shown that the world produces enough grain to provide every person with sufficient protein and about 3,000 calories a day, about the average American's caloric intake.[36] (One-third of the world's calories is presently fed to animals.) The 3,000-calorie estimate does not even include the fruits, vegetables, nuts, root crops, and non–grain-fed meat that are produced around the world.

Georg Borgstrom, author of *The Hungry Planet,* points out the protein-starved underdeveloped countries actually export more protein to wealthy nations than they receive. He calls this "the protein swindle." Ninety percent of the world's fish meal catch, for example, is exported to rich countries. Borgstrom states:

> Sometimes one wonders how many Americans and Western Europeans have grasped the fact that quite a few of their beef steaks, quarts of milk, dozens of eggs, and hundreds of broilers are the result, not of their agriculture, but of the approximately two million metric tons of protein, mostly of high quality, which astute Western businessmen channel away from the needy and hungry.[37]

Military Spending

A frequently overlooked cause of global hunger is military spending. The world's current annual military budget is $600 billion, an amount equal to the total yearly income of the poorer half of the world's people.[38] The arms race diverts precious resources away from productive activities and basic human needs. During 1980 and 1981, about one-third of the total world industrial capacity was used for military production.[39] Twenty-five percent of worldwide research money was used for military research.[40] About 10 percent of the world's total annual output of certain important minerals is used for direct military purposes.[41] Perhaps the situation was best summed up in 1981 by this statement by the Archbishop of Canterbury:

> It is vital that we see modern weapons for what they are, evidence of madness. . . . This is a world where children are dying of hunger while we continue to pour our best efforts into preparing for Armageddon.[42]

Additional negative effects of the arms race on poor countries will be discussed in the next chapter.

Response to Hunger

Judaism teaches involvement and concern with the plight of fellow human beings. Every life is sacred, and we are obliged to do what we can to help others. The Torah states that "Thou shalt not stand idly by the blood of thy neighbor", (Leviticus 19:16).

We speak out justifiably against the silence of the world when 6 million Jews and 5 million other people were murdered in the Holocaust. Can we be silent when millions die agonizing deaths due to lack of food? Can we acquiesce in the apathy of the world to the fate of starving people?

Elie Wiesel has pointed out that there can be no analogies to the Holocaust, but that it can be used as a reference. In that context, we can compare the 10 million children who die each year due to malnutrition with the 6 million Jews slaughtered by the Nazis. True, these children are not bring singled out because of their religion, race, or nationality, but, like the Holocaust victims, they die while the world goes about its business, grumbling about "soaring inflation" and personal inconveniences, indifferent to the plight of the starving masses. And yet the Talmud teaches that if one saves a single human life, it is as if one has saved a whole world. What then if one permits a single life to perish? Or 10 million?

The Hebrew prophets berated those who were content and comfortable while others were in great distress.

Tremble, you women who are at ease,
Shudder, you complacent ones,
Strip and make yourselves bare,
Gird sackcloth upon your loins.
Isaiah 32:11

Woe to those who are at ease in Zion . . .
Woe to those who lie upon beds of ivory and stretch themselves
    upon their couches. . .
Who drink wine from bowls,
And anoint themselves with the finest oils,
But are not grieved at the ruin of Joseph.
Amos 6:1, 4,6

During the Holocaust, many people had rationalizations to justify their silence. Jewish history and ethical teachings should sensitize us to the necessity of speaking out and acting in ways that will reduce the scandal of world hunger.

Action Ideas

What can and should be done to combat the staggering problem of global malnutrition?

First, we must become aware of the real causes of world hunger, This means breaking through the many myths surrounding this issue to realize that hunger is not due to too many people, scarcity of land, lack of technology, backwardness and laziness of native people, or bad weather. It means knowing that giving up a hamburger or fasting once a week can be of some help but does not attack prime causes. It means being aware that hunger is a scandal due primarily to injustice and inequality and that reducing hunger requires fundamental changes in social, political, and economic conditions.

Once the problem is understood, it is important to help inform others. Within the Jewish community, rabbis can deliver sermons on the issue and principals of religious schools can see that children become aware of world hunger and appropriate Jewish responses. Within synagogues, small groups can be established to investigate hunger issues, and hunger-awareness events can be held. It is also important to write letters to newspapers and political leaders.

U.S. public policy on hunger must be changed. Out of seventeen developed nations, we have been fourteenth from the top (in terms of percent of GNP) in supplying food and developmental aid to poor countries.[43] Most of the aid has been for strategic and military reasons, to reduce surpluses, and to create future markets for our agricultural products.

We should work to increase our aid to poor countries, but aid should generally not be in the form of direct food grants. These can worsen conditions in hungry countries by lowering food prices and forcing local small farmers out of business. Aid should be in terms of educational and technical assistance that will help people and groups to become self-reliant. This is consistent with Maimonides' concept of the highest form of *tzedakah:* to help a person so that he can survive through his own efforts. There is a popular saying that "if you give a person a fish, he has a meal for a day; if you teach him how to fish, he has meals for many days."

We must stop supplying military and counterinsurgency aid to repressive regimes that prevent changes necessary to improve the lot of the people. Such aid is used to intimidate, imprison, and torture the poor who are working to free themselves from hunger. We should work to insure that any government that receives U.S. foreign aid is promoting more equitable distribution of control over land and other resources. We should attempt to direct U.S. government help toward limiting the role of agribusiness in food economies here and in underdeveloped countries.

We must make major efforts to move toward a more peaceful world. Money diverted from an insane arms race could be used for the development so essential to reducing poverty and malnutrition in most of the countries of the globe. In 1977, former U.S. Secretary of Defense Robert S. McNamara said, "It always comes down to a question of priorities: a new generation of fighters for the air force or a new generation of infants who will live beyond their fifth birthday."

We should look toward models for farm production such as the Israeli kibbutz (a voluntary collective farm where the income is shared and work and authority are rotated) as an approach enabling farm workers to govern their own lives and share the produce of their work fairly. The Chinese village of Tachai was changed from a mountainous wasteland to a producer of more food than required, due to the collective work of the peasants. The villagers found that cooperative work could produce greater yields than their fragmented and inefficiently operated private plots.[44]

Changes in Life-styles

There is a need to simplify our life-styles and reduce our consumption of food and other resources. As Sister Elizabeth Seton stated, we should "live simply that others may simply live."

An outstanding group of religious leaders, including representatives of various branches of Judaism from the U.S. and Israel, met in Bellagio, Italy, in May 1975 to consider "The Energy/Food Crisis: A Challenge to Peace, A Call to Faith." They agreed on a statement that included this assertion:

The deepest and strongest expression of any religion is the "styles of life" that characterizes its believers. It is urgent that religious communities and individuals scrutinize their life style and turn from habits of waste, overconsumption, and thoughtless acceptance of the standards propagated by advertisements and social pressures.

The cry from millions for food brought us together from many faiths. God—reality itself—calls us to respond to the cry for food. And we hear it as a cry not only for aid but also for justice.

Simpler life-styles, including less wasteful diets, can be an important first step toward justice for the hungry of the world. And simpler diets do not imply a lack of joy, a lack of fellowship. As Proverbs states, "Better a dinner of herbs where love is than a stalled ox with hatred" (15:17).

During the Middle Ages, some local Jewish councils set up "sumptuary laws" for the community; people were forbidden to spend more than a limited amount of money at weddings and other occasions. These laws were designed so that the poor should not be embarrassed at not being able to match expenditures of the wealthy, and to avoid financial strain on the community as a whole. Perhaps the spirit of such laws should be invoked today. Can we continue to consume flesh, which wastes so much grain, at a time when millions are starving? Is it now time for rabbis to specify guidelines to reduce waste and ostentation at weddings, bar mitzvahs, and other occasions?

Can a shift to vegetarian diets make a difference with regard to world hunger? Consider these statistics:

1. Two hundred and forty million Americans are eating enough food (largely because of high consumption of grain-fed livestock) to feed over 1 billion people in the poor countries![45]

2. The world's cattle consume an amount of food equivalent to the calorie requirements of 8.7 billion people.[46]

3. If the average U.S. citizen were to reduce consumption of meat and poultry by 10 percent, 12 million or more tons of grain would become available for food.[47]

These facts indicate that the food being fed to animals in the affluent nations could, if properly distributed, end both hunger and malnutrition throughout the world. A switch away from flesh-centered diets would free land and other resources that could be used to grow nutritious crops for people. It would then be necessary to promote policies that would enable people in the underdeveloped countries to use their resources and skills to become food self-reliant.

It is interesting to note that the first biblical dietary law was vegetarian:

> And God said: "Behold I have given you every herb yielding seed which is upon the face of all the earth, and every tree, in which is the fruit of a tree yielding seed—to you it shall be for food.
>
> Genesis 1:29

While permission to eat meat was later given (Genesis 9:3), Rabbi Abraham Kuk, the first chief rabbi of prestate Israel and others felt that this was a concession to people's weakness and that God would prefer people to be vegetarians. He felt that the many restrictions related to the preparation and consumption of meat imply a scolding and are designed to keep alive the concept of reverence for life and to eventually lead people back to a vegetarian diet. Rav Kuk felt that in the days of Messiah, people would again exist on a nonflesh diet. He based this on the prophecy of Isaiah:

> And the wolf shall dwell with the lamb,
> And the leopard shall lie down with the kid;
> And the calf and the young lion and the fatling together; . . .
> And the lion shall eat straw like the ox. . . .
> They shall not hurt nor destroy in all My holy mountain.
>
> Isaiah 11:6–9

A detailed analysis of this topic can be found in the author's *Judaism and Vegetarianism* (published by Exposition Press).

The means are available for everyone to have an adequate diet. Every nation could be self-sufficient in producing food. The conditions of inequality and injustice that are causing widespread hunger are scandalous and must be changed. As Mahatma Gandhi stated, "There is enough for the world's need but not for its greed."

In a world full of hunger, poverty, and injustice, explicit Jewish mandates to feed the hungry, help the poor, share resources, practice *tzedakah,* show compassion, and pursue justice, and our own experience of oppression throughout Jewish history teach that we cannot stand by idly while millions of our fellow humans lack adequate diets. We must be actively involved in efforts to create a food-production and distribution system consistent with Jewish values such as "the earth is the Lord's" and the sanctity of every life.

Chapter 7

Peace

All that is recorded in the Torah is written for the sake of peace; and although warfare is recorded in the Torah, even warfare is recorded for the sake of peace.

—Tanchuma, Tzav 3

Mere praise of peace is easy and ineffective. What is needed is active participation in the fight against war and everything which leads to it.

—Albert Einstein

The threat of nuclear holocaust is the most critical issue facing humanity today. As more and more nations obtain modern weapons and as the power and accuracy of these weapons increase, the security of every person is threatened.[1]

There are now 50,000 nuclear weapons in the world. (The U.S. has about 30,000 and the Soviet Union about 20,000.)[2] The U.S. and the Soviet Union presently have a combined total of 3½ tons of TNT in explosive power for every man, woman, and child on earth.[3] The world currently has over 6,000 times the total destructive power used in World War II, including the Hiroshima and Nagasaki atomic bombs.[4] The U.S. can destroy the Soviet Union fifty times, and they have comparable power. It has been estimated that a nuclear war could kill 140 million Americans, 113 million Soviet people, and 100 million Europeans.[5]

Although former secretary of defense Robert McNamara estimated that 400 nuclear weapons were sufficient for either country to have as an effective deterrent,[6] the U.S. has over 12,000 nuclear weapons that can reach the Soviet Union and they have almost 8,000 nuclear weapons that can reach the U.S.[7] In his 1979 State of the Union message, President Carter stated, "Just one of our relatively invulnerable *Poseidon* submarines—comprising less than 2 percent of our total nuclear force—carries enough warheads to destroy every large and medium-sized city in the Soviet Union."[8] Yet each year, the Pentagon and its Russian counterpart seek ever more sophisticated, deadly, and expensive weapons.

The nations of the world are placing increasing reliance on arms. It is expected that within a decade, about thirty-five countries, many with unstable governments, and perhaps terrorist groups will have a capability to produce nuclear weapons,[9] greatly increasing the chances of nuclear war by miscalculation or accident. Economist Robert Heilbroner has predicted that nuclear weapons may be used as a threat to force developed nations to transfer wealth to poverty-stricken countries.[10]

The vast increases in military spending have not made the world more secure. In fact, the opposite has occurred. Recently, nuclear war was almost started on three different occasions due to errors in the U.S. NORAD (North American Air Defense Command) early-warning computer system.[11] On November 9, 1979, bombers were readied when a war-game computer tape was mistaken for a real Soviet attack. Failure of forty-six–cent computer chips triggered three-minute nuclear alerts on June 3 and 6, 1980.[12]

Sidney Lens, military analyst and author, has characterized our time as "The Day before Doomsday."[13] The editors of the highly respected *Bulletin of Atomic Scientists* have recently moved their "Doomsday Clock" from seven minutes to midnight to four minutes to midnight, signifying the greatly increased possibilities of a nuclear conflict.[14]

Call for a Nuclear Freeze

Because of the horrendous nature of current nuclear weapons and the dangers related to some of the weapons currently being planned, there have been many calls for a halt to the nuclear arms race. This would involve a mutual (U.S. and Soviet Union) freeze on the testing, production, and development of nuclear weapons and of missiles and new aircraft designed primarily to deliver nuclear weapons. Advocates of the freeze argue that there is a rough, asymmetrical parity today between the U.S. and the Soviet Union and now is the time to freeze nuclear weapons, before one side gets ahead and a new cycle of nuclear weapons production begins.

The asymmetrical parity has the following form: The USSR has more launchers, more land-based missiles, and greater megatonnage and throw weight; the U.S. has a greater total number of warheads, a better balance of land, sea, and air weapons, greater accuracy, and more advanced technology.[15] In addition, our NATO allies have strategic nuclear weapons, while the Warsaw Pact nations have none.

However, some of the new weapons being planned today have characteristics that could destabilize the present rough parity.[16] The MX missile has a projected accuracy within 300 feet and has the capacity to destroy enemy missiles in hardened silos. *Pershing II* missiles would be the most accurate ballistic missiles in the world. NATO has begun to deploy these missiles in Europe, where they would have a four-to-six-minute flight time to the USSR. The cruise missile is relatively slow but has the capacity to fly low and parallel to the topography below so as to defy radar detection. It is highly accurate. It is easily concealed, so its deployment would make verification of any future nuclear weapons agreement extremely difficult, if not impossible. The *Trident II* missile can deliver fourteen very accurate multiple-targeted warheads. It would be deployed on submarines and therefore invulnerable to attack.

The history of the arms race has generally involved the U.S. developing a new weapons system with the USSR following suit in an average of three or four years. We were first to develop the atomic bomb, the hydrogen bomb, multiple warheads, long-range strategic bombers, high-altitude strategic photo-reconnaissance planes, submarine-launched ballistic missiles, and multiple independently targeted reentry vehicles.[17] Hence, if we develop some of the new, more sophisticated weapons, such as the MX, the cruise missile, and the *Trident II* missile, the Soviet Union would probably soon catch up, and there would be a new level of insecurity, at tremendous economic cost to the world's people.

Besides its destabilizing effects of undermining the present rough U.S.-USSR nuclear parity, the aforementioned new weapons systems would greatly increase the pressure to launch first in a crisis situation, to "use them or lose them." The incentive to develop "launch-on-warning" systems—computer systems that launch attacks based on indications of an enemy attack—would be increased. This would substantially increase the chances of war by error, miscalculation, or misperception. Hence it is urgent that there be a nuclear weapons freeze as soon as possible.

Economic Effects of the Arms Race

There are also many powerful economic arguments for a halt in the nuclear arms race. The world's nations spent about $600 billion in 1983 for the military,[18] an amount equal to the total income of the poorest half of humanity.[19] The U.S. alone has a military budget equal to the income of the poorest quarter of the world's people.[20] It is estimated that the U.S. will spend $1.6 trillion for the military in the next five years.

The world's expenditures on armaments are scandalous, especially when so many human needs are unmet and critical problems face humanity. While there is poverty, malnutrition, illiteracy, disease, and lack of housing in many of the world's countries, the world's military budget continues to increase.[21] As former president Eisenhower said, "Every gun that is made, every warship launched, every rocket fired signifies, in the final sense, a theft from those who hunger and are not fed, those who are cold and are not clothed."[22]

In 1974, the U.S. military spent more in sixteen hours than the U.N. World Health Organization and Food and Agriculture Organization spent in the whole year.[23] In 1978, the world spent about $135 million for international peacekeeping forces and about $400 billion for military uses.[24] Since 1960, donor nations spent a yearly average of five dollars per capita for developmental aid in poor countries and ninety-five dollars per capita for their own military.[25]

Military spending in poorer countries has hindered development. As just one example, Pakistan is spending 80 percent of its annual budget on arms and debt service payments—leaving only 20 percent for all other needs.[26] Yet, in 1982, Pakistan decided it needed $1.6 billion worth of new military equipment from the U.S. Meanwhile most Pakistanis live in mud dwellings and only 25 percent have access to safe drinking water.[27] Arms imports to developing countries soared from $3 billion in 1960 to almost $20 billion in 1979 (both figures given in terms of 1979 dollars).[28]

A heavy defense budget has also hurt the U.S. economy in many ways:

- It has fueled inflation by adding dollars, but not goods and services, into the economy and by diverting scarce resources from productive purposes.
- It has generated unemployment; a billion 1981 dollars applied to the capital-intensive defense industries would create only

28,000 jobs, while this money could create 72,000 jobs in education or 54,000 jobs in health care.[29]

- Military spending has inhibited technological progress and economic growth in civilian industries. Nearly half of America's scientists and engineers have military-related jobs; this shortchanges the development, research, and investment needs of civilian industries.
- The U.S. economy has suffered with regard to that of other countries. Our economy has been plagued by high unemployment, inflation, a weakened dollar, and record balance-of-payment deficits. By contrast, Japan and West Germany, which have concentrated on civilian production, have had relatively prosperous economies.[30] Since 1965, the U.S. has had the lowest rate of productivity growth of any industrial country in the world.

Noted economist John Kenneth Galbraith has pointed out that in a typical year, 1977, the U.S. spent $441 per capita for the military; by comparison, Germany spent $252 per capita and Japan spent $47 per capita.[31] This certainly has much to do with our falling behind these two countries in industrial productivity.

In an op-ed article in the *New York Times,* Seymour Melman, a professor of industrial engineering at Columbia University and author of many books and articles on the arms race, indicated how money spent for arms could be used to strengthen our economy[32]: 7 percent of the proposed military outlays from fiscal 1981 to 1986, $100 billion, could rehabilitate the United States's steel industry so that it would again be the world's most efficient; the $8.4 billion cost overrun, to 1981, on the navy's *Aegis*-cruiser program could be used for the comprehensive research and development effort needed to produce 80- to 100-miles-per-gallon cars; the $11 billion allocated for the cruise-missile programs could bring the annual rate of investment in public works to the 1965 level; and so on.

Today, problems like poverty, illiteracy, crime, pollution, decaying cities, inadequate housing, and crowded hospitals get worse while the money that could help solve them is used for arms.

Jewish Teachings on Peace

The pursuit of peace is a fundamental value in Judaism. The rabbis of the Talmud stated that there are many commandments that require

72

a certain time and place for their performance. But this is not so concerning the mandate of peace, "seek peace and pursue it" (Psalms 34:15): you are to seek it in your own place and pursue it everywhere else (Leviticus Rabbah 9:9).

The famous Talmudic sage Hillel stated that we should "be of the disciples of Aaron, loving peace and pursuing peace" (Pirke Avot 1:12). While Jews frequently went to war in biblical times, they always had a special yearning for peace. The sages stated: "Said the Holy One blessed be He: 'The whole Torah is peace and to whom do I give it? To the nation who loves peace!' " (Yalkut Shimoni, Yithro 273).

The rabbis of the Talmud used lavish words of praise to indicate the significance of peace:

> Great is peace, for God's name is peace, as it is said (Judges 6:24), "And he called the Lord peace". . . . Great is peace, for it encompasses all blessings. . . . Great is peace, for even in times of war, peace must be sought [Leviticus Rabbah 9:9].
>
> Great is peace, seeing that when the Messiah is to come, he will commence with peace, as it is said [Isaiah 52:7], "How beautiful upon the mountains are the feet of the messenger of good tidings, that announce peace" [Leviticus Rabbah 9:9].
>
> If Israel should worship idols, but she be at peace, God could not (so to speak) punish them [Genesis Rabbah 38:6].
>
> The whole Torah was given for the sake of peace, and it is said [Proverbs 3:17], "all her paths are peace" [Gittin 59b].

While there are many sections in the Bible that justify war under certain conditions and discuss rules for combat, the general trend is to condemn war and its instruments. God is often pictured as hating war:

And I will break the bow and the sword and the battle out of
    the land,
And will make them to lie down safely.

Hosea 2:20

He maketh wars to cease unto the end of the earth;
He breaketh the bow, and cutteth the spear in sunder;
He burneth the chariot in the fire.

Psalm 46:10

It is of great significant that many of the most important Jewish prayers end with a supplication for peace. These include the Amidah (silent prayer recited three times daily), the Kaddish, the Grace after meals, and the priestly blessing.

The Talmudical sages forbade the use of instruments of war for ornamentation or anything connected with sacred services. Related to the Sabbath laws, the Mishnah states:

> [On the Sabbath] a man may not go out with a sword, a bow, a shield, a club, or a spear; and if he went out [with such as these] he is liable to a sin offering. Rabbi Eliezer says: They are merely decorations. But the sages say: They are nothing but shameful.
>
> Shabbat 6:4

The Talmud regards the sword as the enemy of the Torah: "If the sword is here, there cannot be the book; if the book is here, there cannot be the sword" (Avoda Zarah 17b).

To the Talmud, the true hero is not the person with many conquests:

> He who conquers his impulses, it is as if he conquered a city of heroes. . . . For the true heroes are the master of Torah, as it is said, "mighty in power are those who obey His Word."
>
> Avot de R. Nathan 51:27

> Who is mighty? He who controls his passions, as it is said [Prov. 16:32]: "Better is the long suffering than the mighty. . . ."
>
> Pirke Avot 4:1

The Torah forbids the use of metal tools in the construction of the Holy altar. "And if thou make Me an altar of stone, thou shalt not build it of hewn stones; for it thou lift up thy tool [literally *sword*] upon it, thou hast profaned it" (Exodus 20:25). Consistent with their abhorrence of war, the sages commented on this verse as follows:

> Iron shortens life, whilst the altar prolongs it. The sword, or weapons of iron, is the symbol of strife, while the altar is the symbol of reconciliation and peace between God and man, and between man and his fellow.
>
> Sifra Kedoshim 11:8

Because of his many military activities, King David was denied the opportunity to build the Temple. He was told:

> You have shed blood abundantly, and you have made great wars. You shall not build a house unto My name, because you have shed much blood upon the earth in My sight. Behold, a son shall be born to you who shall be a man of peace; and I will give him

rest from all his enemies round about, for his name shall be
Solomon (peaceful), and I shall give peace and quiet to Israel in
his days. He shall build a house for My name. . . .

1 Chronicles 22:8–9

In spite of the great yearning in the Jewish tradition for peace,
there have been wars through history, up to our own day.

The prophets realized the horrible results of battle. The following
words of Jeremiah (4:19–27) could have been said about the aftermath
of nuclear war:

My bowels, my bowels! I writhe in pain!
The chambers of my heart!
My heart moaneth within me!
I cannot hold my peace!
Because thou hast heard, O my soul, the sound of the horn,
The alarm of war.
Destruction follows upon destruction;
For the whole land is spoiled; . . .

I beheld the earth,
And, lo, it was waste and void;
And the heavens, and they had no light.
I beheld the mountains, and lo, they trembled.
And all the hills moved to and fro.
I beheld, and, lo, there was no man,
And all birds of the heavens were fled.
I beheld, and, lo, the fruitful field was a wilderness,
And all the cities thereof were broken down
At the presence of the Lord,
And before his fierce anger.

For thus saith the Lord:
"The whole land shall be desolate."

The prophets envisioned a time when the instruments of war would
be converted into tools of production:

And they shall beat their swords into plowshares,
and their spears into pruning hooks;
Nation shall not lift up sword against nation,
Neither shall they learn war any more.
But they shall sit every man under his vine and under his
    fig-tree;

And none shall make them afraid;
For the mouth of the Lord of hosts has spoken.
                    Micah 4:3,4; Isaiah 2:4

However, the world's people are currently, in effect, beating plowshares into swords, pruning-hooks into spears.

Causes of War

Judaism teaches that violence and war result directly from injustice.

> The sword comes into the world because of justice delayed, because of justice perverted, and because of those who render wrong decisions.
>   —Pirke Avot 5:11

Judaism emphasizes that justice and harmonious relations among nations reduce violence and prospects for war. The prophet Isaiah states (32:17):

> And the work of righteousness shall be peace;
> And the effect of righteousness quietness and confidence forever.

The Psalmist indicates (Psalm 85:11):

> When loving-kindness and truth have met together,
> then righteousness and peace have kissed each other.

The Talmudic rabbis stress that justice is a precondition for peace:

> The world rests on three things: on justice, on truth, and on peace. And all three are one, for where there is justice, there is also truth, and there is peace.
>   Pirke Avot 1:18; Taanit 4:2

The Hebrew word for war, *milchama,* is derived from the word *locham,* which, interestingly, means both "to feed" as well as "to wage war." The Hebrew word for bread, *lechem,* comes from the same root. This led the sages to suggest that the lack of bread and other essential resources leads to war. The seeds of war are often found in the inability of a nation to provide adequate food for its people. Hence the tremendous amounts of grains fed to animals raised for slaughter, which could be used to feed starving people, could be a prime cause for war.

Sen. Mark Hatfield of Oregon has stated:

Hunger and famine will do more to destabilize this world; it's more explosive than all atomic weaponry possessed by the big powers. Desperate people do desperate things. . . . Nuclear fission is now in the hands of even the developing countries in many of which hunger and famine are most serious.[33]

Richard J. Barnet, a director of the Washington-based Institute for Policy Studies and author of *The Lean Years,* an analysis of resource scarcities, believes that by the end of the century, the anger and despair of hungry people could lead to acts of terrorism and economic class wars.[34]

Just as scarcity of food can lead to war, so can scarcity of sources of energy. A prime current threat to peace is the necessity for affluent countries to obtain sufficient oil to keep their economies running smoothly. The Persian Gulf area, where much of the world's oil is produced, is a place where there has been much recent instability and competition between the superpowers, which could result in war.

Hence, according to the Jewish tradition, it is essential to work for more just conditions, with less waste and more equitable sharing of resources, to reduce the chances of war or violence. This means working to change economic and production systems that are based on waste, exploitation of people, and the keeping of the majority of the world's people in poverty.

Judaism on Treatment of Enemies

Judaism has very powerful statements about how enemies should be regarded:

Rejoice not when your enemy falls,
And let not your heart be glad when he stumbles. . . .
Proverbs 24:17

If your enemy is hungry, give him bread to eat,
And if he is thirsty, give him water to drink.
Proverbs 25:21

77

God is pictured as feeling compassion even for the enemies of the Jewish people:

> In that hour when the Israelites crossed the Red Sea [after the waters drowned the Egyptians],
> The ministering agents wanted to sing a song of praise before God.
> But He said to them: "My handiwork is drowning in the sea, yet you want to sing a song before me!"
>
> Sanhedrin 39b

When celebrating Passover, the commemoration of the exodus from Egypt, Jews temper their celebration, because Egyptians died during that event. This is reflected in two Passover observances:

- At the Seder table, one drop of wine is spilled at the recitation of each of the ten plagues, to reduce our joy (wine symbolizes joy) by at least ten drops.
- The complete Hallel, hymns of praise to God, is recited on only the first two days of Passover. On the rest of the holiday, only half of Hallel is said (because the crossing of the sea and drowning of the Egyptians took place on the last days). On Sukkot, by contrast, the entire Hallel is recited the whole week.

Judaism does not believe that another person or nation need be considered a permanent enemy. Under the right conditions, changes can occur.

> Who is the mightiest of heroes? He who makes of his enemy his friend.
>
> Avot de Rabbi Nathan, chapter 23

Judaism believes that forebearance to adversaries can lead to understanding and eventually to conciliation. Many statements in the Jewish tradition point to ways of eventually establishing reconciliation with enemies.

> Say not thou, I will pay back evil.
> Proverbs 20:22

> When a man's ways please the Lord, he maketh even his enemies to be at peace with him.
>
> Proverbs 16:7

The following story epitomizes the Jewish stress on converting an enemy into a friend. Samuel ibn Nagrela, a Spanish Jewish poet of the eleventh century, was vizier to the king of Granada. One day a certain man cursed Samuel in the presence of the king. The king commanded Samuel to punish the offender by cutting out his tongue. However, Samuel treated his enemy kindly, whereupon the curses became blessings. When the king next saw the offender, he was astonished to note that Samuel had not carried out his command. When asked why not, Samuel replied, "I have torn out his angry tongue and given him instead a kindly one."[35]

By treating an enemy like a human being created in God's image, entitled to respect and sometimes in need of help, we can often obtain a reconciliation. Based on the biblical verse that "if thou see the ass of him that hatest thee lying under its burden, thou shalt forebear to pass by him; thou shalt surely release it with him" (Exodus 23:5), a Talmudical sage finds the following lesson:

> Rabbi Alexandri said: Two ass-drivers who hate each other travel on the road. The ass of one of them falls under its burden and his companion by-passes him. But then he says to himself: "It is written in the Torah: "If thou see the ass of him that hatest thee lying under its burden, thou shalt forebear to pass by him, thou shalt surely release it with him." He immediately turns back and helps his fellow to reload. The other ass-driver then begins to meditate in his heart, saying, "This man is really my friend and I did not know it." Both then enter an inn, and eat and drink together.
>
> Tanchuma Mishpatim 1

Philo, the great Jewish philosopher who lived in Alexandria, Egypt, in the first century of the common era also interpreted the above biblical passage in terms of an attempt to reconcile enemies. He wrote that, by fulfilling it,

> you will benefit yourself more than him: he gains an irrational and possibly worthless animal, you the greatest and most precious treasure, true goodness. And this, as surely as the shadow follows the body, will be followed by a termination of the feud. He is drawn toward amity by the kindness which holds him in bondage. You, his helper, with a good action to assist your counsels, are predisposed to thoughts of reconciliation.[36]

The Talmud teaches that "If two people claim thy help, and one is the enemy, help him first" (Baba Metzia 32b). This is based on the importance of converting an enemy into a friend.

It is significant that our staunchest foes often later become our allies. Germany and Japan, both bitter enemies of the U.S. during World War II, are now considered important trading and military partners of the U.S. While there was talk about "nuking China" not too long ago, we are now negotiating with them about arms sales. Our present enemy, the Soviet Union, was of tremendous help in World War II in stopping the Nazi advance through Eastern Europe. They also provided great assistance to Israel by providing, through Czechoslovakia, desperately needed arms to Israel during her War of Independence. Hence the "demonization of enemies" would appear to be inconsistent with both Jewish values and recent world history.

The Soviet "Threat"

Many people may agree that the nuclear arms race must be halted soon and then ask, "But what about the Russians? Can we trust them? Won't they continue to expand if we don't increase our military strength? Aren't they already ahead of us?"

There have been many claims that the Russians are surpassing us militarily so we must increase our defense spending. But the Washington-based Center for Defense Information, a group composed largely of retired American admirals and generals, has shown that the U.S. and its NATO allies and China have far more strategic nuclear weapons, military spending, military personnel, and major surface ships than the Soviet Union and its Warsaw Pact allies.[37] They point out that the myth of American weakness is a major threat to the United States today, and ignorance of the USSR undermines effective U.S. foreign and military policies. They state further that the Soviet leaders face innumerable foreign and domestic problems and more severe problems of national defense than the U.S. does. After assessing an aggregation of military and nonmilitary factors, they conclude that "the balance of world power is strikingly to the advantage of the West and its allies."[38]

Many U.S. military leaders agree with this assessment. In 1981, the chief of staff of each of the services was asked whether he would trade his service—its weapons, personnel, overall range of capabilities, strengths, and weaknesses—for its Soviet counterpart service. The admiral and each of the generals said they would not make such a trade.[39] Admiral Thomas Hayward, chief of naval operations, stated:

> I would not trade the U.S. Navy for the Soviet Navy under any circumstances. Our forces today are modern and sophisticated, embodying some of the most advanced technology American industry can produce. Our capabilities are improving over the full spectrum of navy warfare. . . .[40]

Gen. Lew Allen, air force chief of staff, stated:

> I would not trade the U.S. Air Force for its Soviet counterpart. Our people are better motivated, trained, and educated than their Soviet counterparts, and in most areas the quality of our weaponry is unsurpassed. . . . There is no question that the U.S. Air Force is the finest in the world.[41]

Harold Brown, former secretary of defense, said on July 20, 1980:

> I believe that those who mistakenly claim that the United States is weak or that the Soviet Union is strong enough to run all over us are not only playing fast and loose with the truth, they are also playing fast and loose with U.S. security.[42]

Recently *The Nation* investigated U.S. and Soviet military strength, and concluded:

> The claim of high Soviet military spending mainly rests on the statistics compiled by the Central Intelligence Agency. When the C.I.A.'s distortions are accounted for, the United States is shown to be spending substantially more than the Soviet Union, and the NATO Alliance as a whole far more than the Warsaw Treaty Organization. As played by the C.I.A. and the Administration, [the military numbers game] aims to mislead the public so as to win support for a new, dangerous round in the arms race.[43]

One factor frequently overlooked in comparing U.S. and Soviet military strength is our vastly superior technology. Our weapon systems have a substantial lead in accuracy, reliability, readiness, and lethality. According to Adm. Gene LaRocque (Ret.) of the Center for Defense Information, U.S. strategic forces have 95 percent readiness, compared to 75 percent for the Soviet Union.[44] The reliability (probability of missile mission completion) is 80 percent for the U.S. and 65 percent for the Soviets.[45] While the Soviet Union has bigger bombs (more megatonnage), American warheads have much greater destructive power, due to superior accuracy.

In assessing Soviet military expenditures and manpower, the following factors should also be considered:

- The Soviet military (and economic) system is very inefficient. According to a 1977 International Institute for Strategic Studies report, 90 percent of the Soviet military budget increase "stems from inefficiency."[46]
- Anti-Soviet nations (the U.S., other NATO countries, and China) lead the Soviet Union and its Warsaw Pact allies in four major military indicators: strategic nuclear weapons (10,500 compared to 7,800), military spending ($298 billion to $202 billion), military personnel (9.7 million to 4.8 million) and major surface warships (435 to 281).[47]
- Although the Warsaw Pact does have more tanks in Europe than NATO (26,000 compared to 17,000), NATO leads in military spending ($242 billion to $202 billion), naval aircraft (1,153 to 774), antitank guided weapons launchers (5,800 to 1,400), and total ground forces in Europe (2,123,000 to 1,669,000).[48]
- The Kremlin faces far greater stategic problems than Washington does. It must prepare against a nuclear threat not just from the U.S., but from several other countries. While Cuba is our only hostile neighbor, the Soviet Union is surrounded by foes with ideological and territorial grievances.

Hillel taught: "Do not judge another person until you have been in his place" (Pirke Avot 2:5). One of the prime causes of difficulty in the world today is that people assume their country is completely right and their opponent completely wrong. They assume other nations' actions are based only on selfish interests, while their own country is always altruistic.

In the spirit of Hillel, while deploring the Soviet system and many of its brutal actions, let us try to understand why the leadership and people of the Soviet Union may have genuine apprehension concerning our country and our allies. It is important to make this analysis in order to "seek and pursue" peace.

The Soviets are dominated by fear of invasion. Historically, they have the lesson of Napoleon and, even more recently, the memory of vast armies penetrating their homeland during World War II. They frequently have ceremonies to honor the memory of over 20 million of their countrymen who died in that war. War memorials are widespread throughout the country. A small Western force, including U.S. soldiers, also invaded them in 1918, after their revolution and World War I.

As viewed by Kremlin leaders, the world must seem very frightening. They know that the U.S. has 10,000 long-range strategic nuclear warheads, over half of them on virtually invulnerable submarines. They realize that the U.S. controls the seas. They must worry about the loyalty of their satellite nations. Recently, their troops have been bogged down in Afghanistan and they have had to impose repressive measures in Poland to avoid the introduction of democratic procedures.

The hostility of China means that over a half-million Soviet soldiers must be kept on the tense border with that nation. Soviet client states such as Angola, Afghanistan, Cuba, Ethiopia, and South Yemen are short of many resources and thus drain the Soviet economy.

Many Americans fear that geopolitical momentum is on the side of the Soviet Union. However, a comprehensive study by the respected Center for Defense Information does not support perceptions of Soviet advances and devastating U.S. setbacks. Outside Eastern Europe, Soviet influence has lacked staying power. They now have influence in only about 12 percent of the world's nations.[49] They have gained support recently mainly among the world's poorest and most desperate countries. Recent Soviet setbacks in China, Indonesia, Egypt, India, and Iraq have dwarfed marginal Soviet advances in less-developed countries.

It is urgent that the U.S. understand that these Soviet fears can make them more dangerous. We must take steps to eliminate or at least minimize their apprehensions by striving for the widest possible cooperation and understanding and a mutual reduction in deadly weapons.

What about Soviet- and Cuban-sponsored effects to promote Communism in many countries? Certainly they would like to see their system in practice throughout the world. But we should consider two factors:

- To back our perceived national interests, the U.S. government has also intervened directly or indirectly in many countries, on an average of once every eighteen months.[50] These included: Greece, 1948; Iran, 1953; Guatemala, 1954; Indonesia, 1958; Lebanon, 1958; Laos, 1960; Cuba, 1961; the Congo, 1964; Guyana, 1964; the Dominican Republic, 1965; Chile, 1973; Vietnam and Cambodia, the 1960s and early 1970s; El Salvador, Nicaragua and Grenada in the 1980s. As Rev. William Sloane Coffin has stated, both the U.S. and the USSR have much to confess with regard to our foreign policies.

- The best way to halt the spread of Communism is not through providing dictators with increasing amount of weapons.[51] It is by eliminating unjust conditions—oppression, poverty, ignorance, and squalor—that lead people to look to Communism as their savior. Instead of spending greater amounts on arms, we can use money saved from military spending to help poorer countries develop their economies and build strong, stable, democratic governments.

There are many reasons to believe that the Soviet Union would welcome American initiatives toward a halt in the arms race. Additional expenditures on arms do not increase their security. They badly need the money now being spent on increasingly costly weapons to meet domestic needs. There is a general consensus that an essentially rough equivalence now exists between U.S. and Soviet forces. Since a higher percentage of their missiles (compared to ours) are land-based, they are much more vulnerable to attack. The Soviet people have painful memories of the horrors of war; scarcely a family was untouched by losses in World War II.

Several times in recent years, the Soviet Union has formally offered to begin negotiations on a comprehensive halt to the nuclear arms race. Unless we put them to the test, we will never know how serious these proposals are.

There is much concern about whether we can trust the Russians to keep an arms agreement. Any pact should not be based on faith in another country's goodwill, but should involve effective internationally controlled supervision. Modern satellites, using high resolution photographs and other sensors, can be used to verify compliance. U.S. detection capabilities are so advanced today that they can read individual automobile license-plate numbers in Moscow.[52] It is thus possible to count and identify individual planes and large missiles on the ground. While it is theoretically possible to secretly produce and stockpile aircraft and missiles, it would be very difficult to do so without telltale signs of construction or supply. Risks of detection would be high, and discovery of violations would incur the world community's condemnation. A report prepared by the Pentagon, Joint Chiefs of Staff, and other federal agencies indicated that Soviet compliance performance under fourteen arms control agreements since 1959 has been good.[53] No system is completely safe, but as former president Kennedy stated, "The risks of peace pale beside the risks of war."

Unfortunately, a powerful segment of the U.S. population has a vested interest in the maintenance of a "Soviet threat" so that military expenditures will continue to increase. One out of every fifty jobs is weapons-related.[54] Over half of our scientists are engaged in military research and development.[55] Two-thirds of the nation's top 100 corporations are heavily involved in the lucrative military market; profit rates are often 15 to 20 percent, or more.[56] The Pentagon funds two lobbyists for every member of Congress and has contracts in as many congressional districts as possible.[57] Military appropriations are the single most important source of investment and profit for corporate America. Hence the struggle to halt the arms race will not be easy, and it will require the skills and determination of many devoted people.

Turning Around the Arms Race

There is general agreement that there is much waste in military spending. The Republican Congressional Study Committee recently estimated that $15 billion a year could be saved if the Defense Department cut duplication, waste, and unneeded arms.[58] The Committee on National Security, a watchdog group of conservative businessmen who favor a strong defense, claim that the military annually wastes $32 billion.[59]

The U.S. already has far more than enough nuclear and conventional weapons on land, under the sea, and in the air to deter any potential attacker. Meanwhile, our security is threatened by budget deficits, lack of a secure energy policy, decaying infrastructures, unsafe cities, ecological dangers, and record balance-of-payment deficits, to name just a few problems.

It is essential that we change our thinking and actions so as to avoid the "unparalleled catastrophe" toward which the world is heading. We must make a start at reducing the arms race. If necessary, we should take some small steps to do this unilaterally, eliminating unnecessary systems while maintaining our security, in the hope that other nations, seeing the folly of an arms race that no country can win, will also start to reduce their arms budgets.

There is a precedent for this: An initiative by President Kennedy in 1963—unilaterally stopping atmospheric nuclear tests—was reciprocated by the Soviet Union in several peaceful actions. There was an atmosphere of reduced international tension, for a short while.

Money saved by cutting military spending can be used to build hospitals and schools, improve mass transit, create jobs, improve the environment, rebuild decaying cities, provide the developmental aid necessary to reduce poverty and hunger, and create an effective world security system—in short, to create a more peaceful and just world.

Efforts to establish a nuclear freeze have been strengthened by support from many religious groups, especially the Catholic bishops, who made a very strong statement urging an end to the nuclear arms race. A cessation in nuclear arms buildup was also unanimously supported by the Synagogue Council of America,[60] an umbrella group composed of rabbinical and congregational organizations of the Orthodox, Conservative, and Reform movements. Recently many Jewish groups have supported a mutual, verifiable halt in the nuclear arms race.[61]

The horrendous weapons possessed by the superpowers mean that there is no sane alternative to peaceful coexistence. Our task cannot be to destroy the Soviet Union or to change its government, but, while refusing to condone its system or actions, to find ways of living side by side with it and dealing with it so as to diminish rather than increase the threats that confront us all.

Consistent with mandates to seek and pursue peace and establish a just world, Jews should be in the forefront of those battling to reverse the world's present path to global holocaust.

Chapter 8

Activism for Peace[1]

"Not by might, not by power, but by my spirit," saith the Lord of Hosts.

—Zachariah 4:6

For thus said the Lord God, the Holy One of Israel:
In sitting still and rest shall ye be saved,
In quietness and in confidence shall be your strength;
And ye would not.
But ye said: "No, for we will flee upon horses";
Therefore shall ye flee;
And: "We will ride upon the swift";
Therefore shall they that pursue you be swift.

—Isaiah 30:15;16

Although Jewish history and religious texts have often included war and reactions to it, the underlying attitude of Jewish tradition is one of abhorrence of violence and an affirmation of the obligation to work and sacrifice for the ultimate goal: peace.

Several statements in the Jewish tradition argue against reliance on military strength. These include[2]:

Because you have trusted in your chariots
And in the multitude of your warriors,
Therefore the tumult of war shall arise among your people,
And all your fortresses shall be destroyed, . . .

Hosea 10:13,14

Some boast of chariots, and some of horses;
But we boast of the name of the Lord our God. . . .
His delight is not in the strength of the horse,
Nor is his pleasure in the legs of a man.
But the Lord takes pleasure in those who fear him,
In those who hope in His steadfast love.

Psalm 147:10–11

The prophets believed that Israel should not depend on military arms and alliances, but

Zion shall be redeemed by justice,
And her returners, by righteousness.
Isaiah 1:27

Jeremiah urged the leaders of Judah to submit to Babylonian invaders, whom he believed to be sent as God's punishment, without a fight (Jeremiah 27:12–14,17), so that the Jewish people would live and continue to carry out God's commandments:

And I spoke to Zedekiah King of Judah according to all these words, saying: "Bring your necks under the yoke of the King of Babylon, and serve him and his people and live. Why will ye die, thou and thy people, by the sword, by the famine, and by the pestilence, as the Lord hath spoken concerning the nation that will not serve the King of Babylon? And hearken not unto the words of the prophets that speak unto you, saying: 'Ye shall not serve the King of Babylon,' for they prophesy a lie unto you. . . . Hearken not unto them; serve the king of Babylon, and live; wherefore should this city become desolate?"

As indicated before, many Jewish teachings extol peace. The Talmudic rabbis indicated that peace is one of God's names, His greatest blessing, and something to be sought and pursued.

While Judaism does recognize the duty of a person to protect his own life and to defend others, it specifically prohibits the shedding of innocent blood:

Murder may not be practiced to save one's life. . . . A man came before Raba and said to him, "The governor of my town has ordered me, 'Go and kill so and so; if not I will slay thee.'" Raba answered him, "Let him rather slay you than that you should commit murder; who knows that your blood is redder? Perhaps his blood is redder."

Sanhedrin 74a

Even in a clear-cut case of self-defense, Judaism condemns the use of excessive violence. The Talmud stresses that if a person being pursued "could save himself by maiming a limb of of the pursuer, but instead kills him," the pursued is guilty of murder (Sanhedrin 74a).

When war was necessary, Judaism still tried to minimize violence. When the Hebrews laid siege to a city in order to capture it, "it may not be surrounded on all four sides, but only on three in order to give an opportunity for escape to those who would flee for their lives."[3] Even in what was considered a just war for defensive purposes, each soldier had to make a sin offering, in recognition that any killing is an offense against God.

To emphasize the value of peaceful relationships, the Talmudic sages radically reinterpreted biblical texts to rid them of their violent aspects. The best example is the life of King David, the great hero of ancient Israel. The Bible focuses on David's character defects and misdeeds related to his use of power. Later, the Talmudic sages reunderstood his character by stressing his creative and contemplative abilities rather than his aggressive characteristics. The rabbis considered him a pious, humble man who spent his time in Torah study and writing psalms, not a military hero.

The Talmud similarly recast the lives of the Jewish patriarchs. Whereas the Bible tells of Abraham leading forth 318 "trained men" to smite those who captured Lot (Genesis 14:14), in the Talmud these men are considered scholars (Nedarim 32a). While Jacob refers to the portions he amassed "with my sword and my bow" (Genesis 48:22), the rabbis interpret Jacob's "sword" to be "prayer" and his "bow" to be "supplication."

Even the character of festivals was modified by the rabbis in order to emphasize spiritual, rather than military power. Originally, Hanukkah celebrated the victory of the Maccabees against the tyranny of the Syrian Greeks. The Talmud deemphasized the military aspects of the victory and stressed the religious aspects of the holiday. Not one word of rabbinic literature extols the Maccabean battles. Thus, for example, when the Talmud described the "miracle which was wrought," it referred to "the oil in the cruse which burned eight days" rather than to "the might of the Hasmoneans (Maccabean army)" (Shabbat 23b).

One of the Talmudic rabbis' favorite statements was "Be of the persecuted rather than the persecutors" (Baba Kamma 93a). Their outlook could be summarized by the following:

> They who are reviled, but revile not others, they who hear themselves reproached but make no reply; they whose every act is one of love and who cheerfully bear their afflictions; these are the ones of whom scripture says: "They who love Him are as the sun going forth in his might."
>
> Yoma 23a; Shabbat 88b; Gittin 36b

The case for nonviolence also finds broad support in Jewish history.

89

Johanan ben Zakkai, a revered teacher of the first century of the common era, is the great hero of Jewish peaceful accommodation. When Rome was besieging Jerusalem, he saw the futility of further Jewish resistance to Roman power. He secretly left Jerusalem and met with the leader of the Roman army. When the Roman general saw his great wisdom, he stated that Johanan could have any wish that he desired. Johanan ben Zakkai chose to establish a school for the study of the Torah at Yavneh. Under his leadership and that of the many brilliant teachers who followed him, a national disaster that could have ended the Jewish people was converted into a new movement for perpetuating Judaism.

From the Roman destruction of the Temple in 70 C.E., until the establishment of modern Israel, with very few exceptions, the Jews as a people never waged war. Without a government, army, or dependent geographical territory to defend, Jews and Judaism survived, not through armed might, but through keeping faithfully to the Jewish tradition and way of life.

There is also a political argument for avoiding war. It is based on the assertion that wars almost never solve international problems but almost invariably result in new and generally greater problems, and that wars invariably breed new wars, each one more destructive than the preceding ones.

The great military hero Napoleon said to his minister of education, "Do you know, Fontanes, what astonishes me most in this world? The inability of force to create anything. In the long run, the sword is always beaten by the spirit."[4]

Another Jewish argument against warfare is related to today's tremendous destructive power. A nuclear war would destroy not only soldiers, but many civilians, either immediately or later (due to radiation). Modern nuclear weapons have the potential of putting an end to humanity, and even other animals, and many species of plants. Considering that Judaism is so scrupulous about shedding innocent blood and about limiting destruction, could Judaism sanction war today?

Yet can a Jew responsibly reject all possibility of violence? Haven't we obligations to others as well as ourselves? Can we simply remain passive before tyranny and injustice? Shall we not defend human values when they are threatened? Can Israel, for example, fail to be militarily strong in the face of antagonism from many of its neighbors?

A pragmatic position consistent with Jewish values today is what Rabbi Albert Axelrad, Hillel Director at Brandeis University, has called the "pacifoid" position.[5] He defines this as one who is "like" or "resembling" or "near" pacifist—that is, a person who joins pacifists in pursuing peace, even while accepting the possibility of fighting if there appears to be no alternative. This would include defending Israel against attack by Arab countries and the Allied resistance to Hitler in World War II.

It must be noted that such a position is not "passivism"—lack of involvement; Jews can act in nonviolent ways in attempting to change unjust conditions. There have been many examples in Jewish history.

Perhaps the first instance of civil disobedience was that of the Hebrew midwives who ignored Pharaoh's command and saved the Israelite male children. The rabbis stated that their action was praiseworthy because the law was genocidal, as well as discriminatory (affecting only Jewish males), and therefore didn't have to be obeyed.

The great medieval philosopher Maimonides held that Jewish law clearly allowed for civil disobedience under certain conditions.

> He who disobeys a king's mandate, because he is engaged in the performance of one mitzvah or another, even an insignificant one, is relieved of guilt . . . and one need not add that if the command itself involves the violation of one of God's mandates, it must not be obeyed!
>
> Mishneh Torah, Hilchot Melakim, 3:9

Can a Jew be a conscientious objector to particular military service based on Torah values? The answer is yes. The prime source for this is Deuteronomy 20:5–8:

> And the officers shall speak unto the people, saying: "What man is there that hath built a new house, and hath not dedicated it? Let him go and return to his house, lest he die in the battle, and another man dedicate it. And what man is there that hath planted a vineyard, and hath not used the fruit thereof? Let him go and return unto his house, least he die in the battle, and another man use the fruit thereof. And what man is there that hath betrothed a wife, and hath not taken her? Let him go and return unto his house, lest he die in the battle, and another man take her." And the officers shall speak further unto the people, and they shall say, "What man is there that is fearful and fainthearted? Let him go and return unto this house, lest his brethren's heart melt as his heart."

In 1970 the Synagogue Council of America, an umbrella of Orthodox, Conservative, and Reform religious groups, indicated in a letter to the director of the Selective Service System, that Jews can claim conscientious objection to war based on their understanding of the moral imperatives of the Jewish tradition:

> Jewish faith, while viewing war as a dehumanizing aberration and enjoining a relentless quest for peace, recognizes that war can become a tragic, unavoidable necessity. Judaism is therefore not a pacifist faith in the sense that this term is generally used.
>
> However, this fact does not preclude the possibility of individuals developing conscientious objection to war based on their understanding of and sensitivity to the moral imperatives of the Jewish tradition. In other words, Jewish faith can indeed embrace conscientious objection, and Jewish religious law makes specific provision for the exemption of such moral objectors.
>
> It is entirely proper for individuals claiming such conscientious objector's status to be questioned about the sincerity and consistency of their beliefs, provided they are not singled out to meet requirements not applicable to members of other faiths. It is entirely improper, however, to reject such applications on the false ground that Judaism cannot embrace conscientious objection.[6]

Similar statements were made by the Rabbinical Assembly (Conservative) in 1934 (reaffirmed in 1941)[7] and by the Central Conference of American Rabbis in 1963.[8] In 1971, the Synagogue Council of America (composed of Orthodox, Conservative, and Reform rabbinic and congregational groups) expanded on previous statements to assert that selective conscientious objection to war is consistent with Judaism:

> . . . Judaism considers each individual personally responsible before God for his actions. No man who violates the eternal will of the Creator can escape responsibility by pleading that he acted as an agent of another, whether that other be an individual or the state. It is therefore possible, under unusual circumstances, for an individual to find himself compelled by conscience to reject the demands of a human law which, to the individual in question, appears to conflict with the demand made on him by a higher law.[9]

What about people who are not pacifists but feel that a certain war is wrong? This became a profound ethical problem when many Americans refused to fight in the Vietnam war because they felt that our involvement was illegal and immoral. This may become an issue again, as the U.S. seems to be moving closer to military involvement in Latin America. The Jewish tradition, which places such great stress on the individual conscience, would seem to be consistent with selective conscientious objector status.

Throughout history, people have generally equated patriotism with blind adherence to their country's policies and willingness to sacrifice their lives for it. Perhaps this is why there have been so many wars—there has never been a shortage of young men willing to unquestioningly "do or die" for their country. Perhaps we need a new broader definition of patriotism, one that asks some tough questions, such as: Is this really best for the people of this country? For the people of the world? Is there no other way to settle our disputes? Is this battle necessary to preserve our ideals and values, or is it to serve corporate interests? Are all the facts known, or have we only heard one side of the issue? Is this likely to lead to a wider war, which would endanger all of civilization? Who stands to gain from this war? Can we change our life-styles to become less wasteful and thus less dependent on resources from other areas in other to reduce our need to go to war? Will this war really solve the problem? Has negotiation been tried?

A group that provides extensive draft registration counseling based on Jewish values is the Jewish Peace Fellowship (see Appendix B).

Peace is Judaism's greatest value. War is humanity's greatest threat. Hence it is essential that Jews be actively involved with others in working for a reduction in deadly weapons, harmony between people and nations, and toward that day when "nations shall not learn war anymore."

Chapter 9

Israel

For Zion's Sake I will not keep silent,
  and for Jerusalem's sake I will not rest,
until her vindication goes forth as brightness,
  and her salvation as a burning torch.
                                    —Isaiah 62:1–2

It shall come to pass in the latter day . . .
That out of Zion shall go forth Torah,
and the word of the Lord from Jerusalem. . . .
                                    —Isaiah 2:2,3

If I forget you, O Jersualem
  let my right hand wither.
Let my tongue cleave to the roof of my mouth
  if I do not remember you,
if I do not set Jerusalem
  above my highest joys.
                                    —Psalm 137:5–6

And I will bring back the captivity of My people Israel, and they
shall build the wasted cities, and dwell therein; and they shall
plant vineyards, and drink their wine; and they shall lay out
gardens and eat their fruit.
                                    —Amos 9:14

As the above quotations affirm, Jews have always cherished Israel.
Even when stateless and dispersed throughout the world, Jews con-
stantly yearned to return to *Eretz Yisrael*. The prayer "Next Year in
Jerusalem," recited at the close of the Yom Kippur service and the
Passover Seder, became a byword among the Jewish people. Now that
Israel exists, Jews consider her as the fulfillment of a dream, a safe

homeland where Jewish tradition and values can be carried out, and a beacon for the world.

Why consider Israel in a book about global survival? Because the unstable situation and the widespread hatreds in the Middle East could result in a conflict leading to nuclear war that could destroy Israel and many other nations; because constant threats to Israel's security preoccupy Jews and keep our attention from other issues related to global survival; because Jews have a special mission to be a "light unto the nations" and methods applied for peace here can serve as models for other world trouble spots. Certainly decisions directly affecting Israel's security must be made by Israelis, but others can contribute to the dialogue about its best options.

Many Jews may feel that people like myself, living safely in the diaspora, should not be speaking out about Israel while she is threatened, especially by discussing policies that sometimes differ from those of Israel's government. They feel that only those whose security is threatened in Israel have a right to express an opinion. However, there are many reasons that Jews should speak out:

- It is not only Israel's survival that is threatened. In the nuclear age, a conflict in the Middle East (or anywhere) potentially threatens every person on earth. Many strategic experts feel that the most likely place for nuclear war to begin is the Middle East.
- There seems to be no objection when Jews espouse views more *right wing* than those of the Israeli government. Apparently, only those who advocate conciliation and compromise are criticized for speaking out. Who has ever challenged the right of Zionist groups or individuals to make hawkish statements publicly?
- There already is an extensive dialogue and debate in Israel on policies with regard to the Arabs, the settlements, et cetera. Hawks in Israel use American support and/or acquiescence as an argument for their side. Hence not speaking out is indirectly backing an Israeli policy. The Israeli Peace Now movement has urged Jews, in Israel and in the diaspora, who question Israel's policies to openly express their views, lest the Israeli government claim that it has unanimous support.[1]
- Judaism stresses discussion and debate as the best way to arrive at correct answers. Only a respectful, open dialogue can lead to an acceptable solution. The most satisfactory answer to an argument is a better argument, not a silencing of opinions. The

strength of democracy is that different opinions may be freely expressed.

- Judaism teaches the special responsibility of helping fellow Jews. When a Jew feels that current policies are harmful to Jews in Israel and better policies should be pursued, how can he or she remain silent?
- Because of our special bond with Israel (consider the United Jewish Appeal slogan, "We Are One"), American Jews have not only the right but the obligation to contribute to Israel's welfare by expressing constructive opinions about what they perceive to be Israel's best interests.
- As indicated in chapter 1, Judaism stresses involvement in critical issues, and dissent and protest when appropriate. The Talmudic principle "Silence is tantamount to agreement" is still pertinent.
- If Jews automatically back every Israeli government policy, their views will not be regarded as sincere, and hence they won't be taken seriously.

It is deplorable that many Jews hold that American Jews must unconditionally support Israel's actions, even if they disagree with them. Accusing Jews who express dissenting opinions of disloyalty to the Jewish people is dangerous to Israel and to Jewish life in the diaspora. Of course, dissent from Israeli policies should be informed and responsible, free from hysteria, and based on love of Jewish values and Israel.

In this chapter, two principles are paramount: Israel must survive with secure, recognized borders, and she must carry out her mission: to be God's witnesses, a kingdom of priests, a light unto the nations, chosen to imitate God's traits of justice, kindness, compassion, and truth.

The Arms Race in the Middle East

Today the Middle East is the world's largest importer of arms; it purchases well over one-third of the world's arms exports.[2] The region is spending over $30 billion annually on its armed forces.[3] It has the world's highest per capita military expenditure and the highest rate of arms growth, increasing over three and one-half times since the 1967 war.[4] Eight of the ten leading arms-importing nations are there.[5]

It is not only the sharp increase in the amount of weapons in the Middle East that is so dangerous; arsenals have also greatly "improved" in quality. The next war could be fought with highly sophisticated electronics, surface-to-surface missiles, laser-guided bombs, drones, and even nuclear weapons. The Stockholm International Peace Research Institute (SIPRI) concluded as far back as 1976 that "the arms buildup in the Middle East shows every sign of being out of control. . . . The continued unrestrained sale of armaments can only exacerbate an already dangerous situation." Since then the arms race in the region has escalated.

The May 1982 issue of the dovish Israeli publication *New Outlook* was devoted completely to "the dangers of nuclear proliferation and confrontation" in the Middle East.[6] Several articles brought out the fact that many countries in this region either have a nuclear weapons capacity or may soon get one, and as former Israeli chief of staff Motta Gur expressed it, "the next Arab-Israeli war, if it occurs, will bring us to the edge of nuclear confrontation." Hence, while Israel may have a temporary advantage in nuclear weapons there is a great need for reconciliation in this volatile area and the establishment of a nuclear-weapons–free zone, before other nations in the area develop these weapons.

Many Jews believe that Israel's security needs require Jewish support for continued U.S. military growth. Certainly Israel's security needs are of urgent importance, but her survival does not require greater U.S. arms spending, for the following reasons[7]:

- There is tremendous waste in U.S. military budgets, which can and should be cut, without any reduction in security. As indicated before, the U.S. can already wipe out the Soviet Union many times, and most U.S. warheads are in virtually invulnerable submarines. The U.S. has a big technical lead in such areas as cruise missiles, warhead accuracy and guidance, submarine detection, computers, and survivability of missiles.
- The U.S. emphasis on the Soviet Union as the biggest threat to the Middle East and other areas has led us to provide sophisticated weapons to many Arab countries. President Reagan's recent decision to send AWACS aircraft to Saudi Arabia is the most recent example. Israel is finding it increasingly difficult to match the billions of Arab oil dollars when it comes to maintaining military superiority.
- Israel is very dependent on continued support from a strong United States; this requires U.S. economic and social well-being. As indicated, large arms expenditures lead to high interest rates, budget deficits, unemployment, and reduced productivity.

If the U.S. economy becomes weaker, American citizens may resent the expenditure of funds for Israel that could otherwise be used to meet local human needs.

- Israel has a strategic advantage in the Middle East for now and the forseeable future. She is regarded as the fourth nation in military strength in the world (behind the U.S., the USSR., and Britain) by the Stockholm International Peace Research Institute.

To insure its security, Israel is spending a staggering amount for arms. Thirty percent of her gross national product goes for the military; this is the highest rate of military spending in the world.[8] Almost a quarter of Israel's population between eighteen and forty-five years of age is employed in the armed forces or military production. The production of military hardware is her leading industry today.

As is true for the U.S. and other countries, Israel's security may ultimately be threatened more by economic and social problems than military problems. In recent years, Israel's heavy military spending has led to intense economic problems such as triple-digit inflation, the world's largest per capita national debt, and an increase in social problems. This has contributed to very high numbers of Israelis leaving the country and a sharp decline in *aliyah* (immigration to Israel). Israel's survival demands a halt to the Middle East arms race.

Middle East Peace

A prime concern of every Israeli is security. The country is small, and its population and industrial centers are close to the borders of potential enemies. Five wars and many skirmishes with hostile neighbors in the last thirty-five years make security a compelling issue for Israelis. While Israel has survived due to military prowess, advanced weapons, excellent intelligence, and a deeply committed citizenry, she must consider how to maintain her security in a time of war-weariness among many of her citizens and the proliferation of increasingly dangerous weapons.

Israel's security and well-being must be preserved. It must have the right to live in peace, within secure borders with her Arab neighbors. This requires an end to terror and violence and the mindless build-up of arms in the area. Israelis and Arabs must seek to understand the measure of legitimacy in each other's views and be willing to seek accommodation. The alternative is disaster for all the region's people.

Israel's security requires acceptance by her Arab neighbors and a political solution with the Palestinian Arabs. This does not mean that Israel should immediately turn over land won in the 1967 war or that it should start to disarm. Hostility and animosity built up over many years cannot be changed quickly. But a start must be made to obtain an equitable settlement that will provide peace, security, and justice for Israelis and Palestinians, for many reasons:

- The absence of direct negotiations between the key parties—Israelis and Palestinians—may result in a "solution" imposed by others. Such an imposed settlement would be geared more to the economic and military interests of competing world powers than to Israeli and Palestinian concerns.
- A continuation of the status quo with additional settlements on the West Bank (Judea and Samaria) will continue to drain the Israeli economy. It will mean increased economic hardships and an inability to address Israel's pressing housing, education, and social problems.
- It is generally recognized that Israel's control over Biblical territory is a result of her defensive action in the Six Day War. However, continued control over Palestinian Arabs in the West Bank and Gaza will lead to harsher measures to retain order, at the expense of Jewish values and Zionist ideals. Already, Bir Zeit, a Palestinian university, has been closed several times, and force has been used to disband Arab protests and demonstrations.
- Israeli society has become severely polarized due to fighting in Lebanon, which resulted in over 500 Israelis killed and 2,000 wounded. At a time when harmony is necessary to meet Israel's many problems, sharp divisions are increasing with regard to Israel's policies toward Arabs. Many Jews have joined protest rallies. There has even been violence among Jews.
- Failure to come to an acceptable settlement will leave Israel with a critical demographic problem: Rapid Arab population growth will lead to an Arab majority in Israel and the West Bank in the relatively near future. Then Israel will be faced with the horrible choice of denying the Palestinians their political rights or seeing them take control of the Israeli government.
- Partly due to the influence of Arab oil, virtually no other country in the world, including the U.S., on whom Israel is critically dependent, approves of Israel's continued control of the territories or disregards the political problem posed by Palestinian

99

nationalism. Israel basically faces the world alone today, and if she continues to maintain her presence in the territories by force, she will find herself increasingly isolated.

- The longer Israel maintains control over and settles the territories, the more difficult it will be to establish peace. Already settlers are armed and organized into paramilitary units, and together with their political supporters within Israel, they promise to strongly resist any return of the land. Recently, Ariel Sharon, former defense minister, stated:

> It is impossible anymore to talk about a Jordanian option or territorial compromise. We are going to have an entirely different map of the country that it will be impossible to ignore. I don't see any way any government will be able to dismantle the settlements of Judea and Samaria.[9]

- For the sake of Israel's security, many Jews have denied fundamental Jewish ethical values and adopted non-Jewish values. Believing that Israel needs American arms help, they have not backed arms control initiatives. Believing that the Soviet Union is the prime troublemaker in the Middle East, they have taken a hard line against détente. Since the Palestinian cause is being supported by the underdeveloped world, many Jews have not been involved in efforts to relieve poverty and hunger in these countries. At a time when the world's critical problems require the involvement of Jews and the application of Jewish values, many Jews have been silent or taken reactionary positions in order to avoid harming Israel.

While a serious obstacle to peace is Arab attitudes and actions, many Israelis believe that Israel should take further initiatives for peace. An Orthodox group, Oz V'Shalom (Strength and Peace), believes that a peace settlement based on territorial compromise is necessary to realize the demands of religious Zionism: the preservation of the Jewish character of Israeli society and the maintenance of the highest ethical standards. They stress that their daily lives and the political life of Israel must be guided by the biblical verse "And thou shalt do what is right and good in the eyes of God" (Deuteronomy 6:18), and the halachic principle "for the sake of peace." They see continued rule over a nationally conscious Arab population as a threat to the internal welfare and ethical character of Israel.

While acknowledging that it takes two sides to make peace, Oz V'Shalom believes that Israel is responsible for a vision of a Jewish state and correct actions in pursuit of that vision. They see the choice as between:

> A Jewish state governed by Biblical values, just laws, and reason *or* a garrison state characterized by chauvinism, institutionalized injustice, and xenophobia; a democratic society, flourishing within small borders, in which the Arab minority enjoys full human dignity and civil rights *or* all of Eretz Yisrael at the price of repressing the political freedom of over 1 million Palestinian Arabs; . . . mutual recognition and co-existence between Israelis and Palestinians *or* escalating destruction and loss of life.[10]

One of Oz V'Shalom's leaders is Uriel Simon, son of the renowned scholar Ernst Simon and professor of Bible at the (Orthodox) Bar Ilan University in Israel. He agrees with Gush Emunim (a primarily religious group formed in 1974 that advocates complete settlement of Judea and Samaria) that Israel has a biblical claim to the territories. However, he feels that a divine promise is not persuasive as a legal document in international relations, especially if it will suppress the freedom of another people.[11] He and other religious Zionists feel that it is the positive ethical and spiritual content of Jewish life and not the size of the state that is most important. Hence they conclude that territorial compromise is the best policy to avoid militarism and chauvinism and to maintain the ethical principles fundamental to Judaism.

What about Jewish law prohibiting Israel from giving back even one inch of ancient Jewish land to the Arabs? According to many Jewish religious authorities, such as Rabbi Ovadiah Yosef, former chief Sephardic rabbi of Israel,[12] Rabbi Immanuel Jakobovits, chief rabbi of England,[13] and Rabbi J. B. Soloveitchik of Boston, a highly esteemed Orthodox rabbi, Zionist, and shaper of religious thought,[14] the concept of "pikuach nefesh"—the duty to save lives—can override territorial considerations. That is, a territorial compromise can be made, if it reduces the chances of future wars, in the opinion of recognized military and strategic experts.

Recently, in the face of Israel's heavy losses in the Lebanese war, there have been additional movements toward more conciliatory positions on the part of Israel's religious community. A new group, Netivot Shalom (Paths of Peace), was formed as a religious dovish answer to Gush Emunim. The group grew out of the Hesder Yeshivot after that movement, which does regular army service, suffered a disproportionate number of casualties in the Lebanon war. About 3,000 Israelis attended the founding meeting of Netivot Shalom, and the group has already had an impact on National Religious party leaders. For example, education minister Zevulun Hammer and deputy foreign minister Yehuda Ben-Meir recently indicated that social issues and the "quality of life" in Israel may be more important than the "quantity" of its land.[15]

Rabbi Yehuda Amital, a Hesder Yeshiva leader, today is one of the foremost advocates that "if there is a chance for peace, Israel should take the risk of territorial compromise."[16] Rabbi Aharon Lichtenstein, one of the rabbis of a Hesder Yeshiva on the West Bank, has stated that "the time has come to declare that there is another school among the religious Zionist public" besides Gush Emunim.[17]

A larger, more secular peace group is Shalom Achshav (Peace Now). They have advocated that Israeli and Palestinian Arab leaders meet to discuss a peace agreement. Peace Now leader Itzhak Galnoor has written:

> Our combined moral and military strength enables us to take the risk involved in seeking peace and agreeing upon borders that are not ideal, but are acceptable to all sides. The security risk can be minimized not through more land, but through security arrangements. Such arrangements may not be foolproof. However, the alternative is more dangerous, because territory becomes a factor inimical to security when its retention involves ruling over another people.[18]

Israeli peace groups and individuals have made many proposals for a peace agenda. Recently Peace Now called on the government of Israel to "take the initiative in breaking the cycle of Israeli-Palestinian hostility and to further the cause of a permanent settlement of the Middle East conflict."[19] Believing that continued rule over a million and a half Arabs distorts the democratic and Jewish character of Israel and impairs the justice and morality of the Zionistic vision, they called on the government of Israel to "conduct negotiations with any Palestinian body which accepts the path of negotiation as the only means of solving the Middle Eastern conflict."[20]

The Peace Now proposal outlined conditions for negotiations, including mutual Israeli-Palestinian recognition, an abandonment of terror by the Palestinians, and discussions based on the Camp David Accords and UN Security Council Resolution 242.[21] Their proposal is based on their belief that "peace can secure borders better than any border can secure peace."[22]

On May 19, 1980, 250 prominent Israelis, among them 5 former generals, 4 former Labor-party government ministers, and 20 current members of Parliament, issued a statement criticizing Israeli "extremists" and urging that Israel seek security "through compromise" on territorial issues. The statement concluded:

> In Israel the Jewish people has sought to guarantee its physical survival, to build a sovereign Jewish society, and to create a spiritual center for the Jewish people.
> Peace is necessary for the full realization of this dream.
> Our way is the way of peace and security through compromise and partition of the land of Israel.
> Our way is the way of coexistence and of tolerance.
> Our way seeks to unite the Jewish people around its Jewish and humanist heritage.
> At this time all those whose way is our way must stand up and be counted. We must build a wall to block violence and we must return to mainstream Zionism.[23]

In a 1983 statement printed in the *Jerusalem Post,* 100 Israeli public figures, including 30 members of Parliament, indicated their belief that the "settlement policy of the present Israeli government is dangerous to the security and future of the state of Israel." Recently, some American Jewish groups such as the Central Conference of American Rabbis and the American Jewish Congress called for a halt to settlements.

In sum, there are many Israelis and diaspora Jews, religious and nonreligious, who are deeply committed to Israel and its security and feel that present Israeli policies are counterproductive and harmful. They believe that Israel should state that it will negotiate with any Palestinian organization that will declare its willingness to recognize the state of Israel and refrain from any hostile activities and terrorism against her. There is no certainty that the Palestinians and Arab states will be willing to end their hostility and live in peace with Israel, but the goal of peace is so essential that this should not be used as an excuse to avoid strenuously seeking reconciliation.

What about the Palestine Liberation Organization? Their unconscionable acts of terror against innocent people, including women and children, must be utterly condemned. The question is how, ultimately, this terrible cycle of terrorism can be ended: only by more force, breeding further violence and hatred? Or, in the end, through a settlement that guarantees each party its most basic human and security needs? Will not these inexcusable acts of violence against innocents—and the desperation that breeds them—continue until we have found a way to achieve self-determination for the Palestinians, as well as justice, peace, and international acceptance for Israel?

Certainly the PLO would prefer Palestinian control over all of Israel. However, there have been some public hints that some Palestinians realize that Israel is here to stay, and that they are willing to compromise and accept a Palestinian state in the West Bank and Gaza in exchange for recognition of Israel's right to live in peace. Of course, Israel cannot be expected to accept empty words and promises: Arab negotiators would have to show by both explicit statements and concrete deeds that they are willing to live in peace and harmony with Israel.

Israel's security must be the utmost concern of every Jew. But Palestinian self-determination and Israel's security are not mutually exclusive; Israel's interests might be best served if the Palestinians achieved self-determination in the context of an agreement guaranteeing Israel's security. Sufficient security guarantees could be written into a peace agreement to bolster Israel's safety. There would be risks, but they would be far less than risks related to the continuation of present policies, with escalating tensions and violence, and arms proliferation.

There are at least four reasons why the foreign policy of a future Palestinian state would tend to be moderate.

- It would initially be involved in organizing a government that would require the consensus of a wide variety of blocs. The job of nation-building and the instinct of political survival would tend to make its leadership prudent in its policies toward Israel, as its incentive toward terrorist activities would be reduced. For the first time, *they* would have something to lose from war, invasion, and mutual destruction!
- The new state would require international as well as Arab economic aid, especially in view of its sparse natural resources. This would give many Western countries leverage in requiring moderate military behavior. Also, the need for the new state to establish and maintain economic contacts with Jordan and Israel would operate as a restraint.
- Israel's overwhelming conventional and nuclear superiority would militate against any conceivable attack by a Palestinian state. The new state would be totally vulnerable to Israel, while Israel would be totally invulnerable. Arab leaders would be acutely aware of the costs of any confrontation with Israel. Any unauthorized military activity by the new state would threaten all its achievements.
- There are several geometric constraints that would frustrate any attack by a Palestinian state. Israel would surround it on three sides and could have strategic highways under constant

observation. The absence of natural barriers such as forests, rivers, or high mountains would make the new state easily accessible to Israel's ground troops and too easily observed for much to be hidden.

To further alleviate Israel's understandable security fears, certain security features could be built into the agreements, such as demilitarized zones, the stationing of international peacekeeping forces for as long as necessary, the use of electronic devices, and the retention of some Israeli military bases.

Retired Israeli general Mattityahu Peled believes that the establishment of a Palestinian state on the West Bank might give Israel a better strategic position than it enjoyed in the pre-1967 period. This is because a negotiated Palestinian state would be militarily weaker than Jordan was when it held the area.[24]

Some of Israel's leaders have realized that security means more than massive military strength and territory. David Ben Gurion, Israel's first prime minister, stated:

> One must not omit any major element in the realm of security: a foreign policy of peace, firm aspiration for peace with our neighbors, with all nations of the world; an active quest for friendly relations with all the large and small nations of the East and West. This policy is in itself an important element of our security.[25]

The following are statements made by Israeli leaders and groups and a Jewish leader in the diaspora about the need for Israeli-Arab reconciliation.

> We Jews who aspire to rebuild our destroyed and dispersed people will respect and honor similar aspirations among other peoples.
> Chaim Weizman, first president of Israel

> A people which rules over another people is not free.
> Peace Now

> Peace is greater than Greater Israel.
> Slogan of Peace Now

> There will never be peace until there is a rapprochement between Israel and the Palestinians.[26]

There are other Jewish values to be considered as well: the mandate to "seek and pursue peace," the concept of converting enemies into friends, and the commandment to pursue justice and reduce poverty and hunger, all of which become secondary while Jews consider Arabs as implacable foes and spend vast amounts on weapons.

Recently some Jewish groups such as Interns for Peace (see Appendix B) and Na'amat Pioneer Woman (Israel's largest women's group)[27] have been working for better relations between Jews and Arabs. But much more needs to be done:

- There should be increased dialogue between Jews and Arabs. This should be extended to all who are concerned about peace in the area.
- The many assumptions that prevent dialogue must be challenged. There must be freedom to express ideas without being labeled anti-Israel or 'disloyal to the Arab cause.'
- There should be a serious scholarly effort to critically examine key arguments and aspects of the conflict.
- Jewish and Arab stereotypes that support existing biases must be overcome.
- There must be greater effort to hear from Israelis and Palestinians who have been working for accommodation. Now, generally, only hard-liners are heard.
- More cooperative projects involving Jews, Arabs, and others are needed.
- Feelings that peace and reconciliation between Jews and Arabs is impossible must be reduced. In the words of early Zionists, "if you will it, it is no dream."

The establishment of peace between Israel and the Arab states will not be easy, but working toward it puts into practice essential Jewish values and mandates: to seek and pursue peace; to turn enemies into friends; to work cooperatively for justice and the preservation of God's world. Among the many blessings of a just Mideast peace would be for Israel to be able to fulfill completely her true moral mission as a living champion of justice, compassion, and, most important, *shalom.*

Chapter 10

International Relations

I saw all the oppressions that are practiced under the sun. Behold, the tears of the oppressed, they had no one to comfort them! On the side of the oppressors there was power. . . .

—Ecclesiastes 4:1

To survey conditions for most of the world's people today is to see the results of ignoring Jewish values and teachings. The tremendous current injustice and inequality are well described by Lester Brown, director of the World Watch Institute:

> In effect, our world today is in reality two worlds, one rich, one poor; one literate, one largely illiterate; one industrial and urban, and one agrarian and rural, one overfed and overweight, one hungry and malnourished; one affluent and consumption-oriented, one poverty stricken and survival-oriented. North of this line (separating the wealthy and the poor), life expectancy closely approaches the Biblical threescore and ten; south of it, many do not survive infancy. In the North, economic opportunities are plentiful and social mobility is high. In the South, economic opportunities are scarce and societies are rigidly stratified.[1]

The social and economic gaps between countries can be demonstrated with many significant statistics comparing the developed countries (U.S., the USSR, Canada, West Germany, England, France, et cetera) and the "developing" countries (Nigeria, India, Bangladesh, Nicaragua, Pakistan, et cetera). The per capita GNP in Switzerland is 120 times that in Bangladesh. An average child born in Iceland can expect to live thirty-six years longer than an average child born in Ethiopia.[2] Almost 20 percent of the babies born in the Gambia don't live until their first birthday, compared to less than one percent for France, Norway, Sweden, the Netherlands, and Denmark.[3] Only 2 percent of the population in Nigeria can expect to live at least sixty-five years, compared to 15 percent in England.[4] Where a person is born in the world certainly makes a difference!

It is difficult for people in wealthy countries to realize the extent of the abject, chronic poverty experienced by so many of our brothers and sisters in the world.

- Poverty means malnutrition. A third to a half of the world's people are undernourished (not enough calories) or malnourished (not enough protein). Over 450 million people are severely and chronically malnourished.[5]
- Poverty means illiteracy. Only 171 million of India's 613 million people were literate in 1975.[6] Typically, less than one person in five is literate in Pakistan, Bangladesh, and many other underdeveloped countries.[7]
- Poverty means sickness and inadequate health care. In the mid-1970s, one-third to one-half of the world's people had no access to health care.[8]
- Poverty means high infant mortality. Over 8 percent of the children born in 1983 died before their first birthday.[9] In some areas, 30 or 40 percent die before they are five years of age.
- Poverty means doing without basic necessities. Economist Robert Heilbroner has outlined what the life-style of a typical family living in an underdeveloped country is like: a minimum of furniture, a minimum of clothes, very crowded conditions, a paucity of food, no running water, no electricity, no newspapers, magazines, or books, perhaps a radio, very few government services, no postman or fireman, perhaps a school three miles away consisting of two classrooms, perhaps a clinic ten miles away, tended by a midwife, and barely any money.[10]

Causes of Poverty

The widespread poverty in the world is primarily due to systems that are completely contrary to Jewish values of justice, compassion, sharing, and love of one's fellow human being.

People in poor countries are not necessarily poor because these countries lack resources. As the script for a slide show, "Sharing Global Resources," expresses it:

Jamaica provides us a wealth of aluminum ore—for cans, military aircraft, industrial equipment.

Why, then, are its people so poor?

And what about that morning cup of coffee? Brazil is the world's largest coffee producer.

Brazil's top 5 percent have increased their share of the national income to 50 percent, according to some estimates.

But what about these Brazilians who pick the coffee beans? Why has the last decade brought Brazil's bottom 40 percent a decline in buying power, worse housing, and poorer food?

South African Blacks mine diamonds, gold, and uranium for the Western world.

Why do four out of five Blacks live in abject poverty? Why do half the children in the Black reserves die before reaching the age of five?

Why has development failed to reach 40 percent of entire populations in the poor world?

And even in the rich world, why is there poverty in Appalachia? One of the most mineral-rich and coal-rich areas of the richest country in the world![11]

For most Third World countries there is a widening gap between what they get for their exports and what they pay for imports. The prices of manufactured goods from industrialized countries go up steadily with respect to raw materials. Hence Third World countries can buy less and less with money they get for raw materials. For example, in 1960, it took only 165 bags of coffee to purchase one tractor; by 1970, it took 316 bags, and by 1977, 400 bags.[12] From 1953 to 1972, raw material prices, excluding oil, decreased by an average of 2 percent per year, compared to manufactured imports.[13] Hence poor countries are on a treadmill and have to work harder and harder to maintain their (inadequate) standard of living.

These unfavorable trade relations produce what is known as the "spiral of debt." It results because the underdeveloped countries are locked in by the economic, political, and military power of wealthy countries. They must export cheap items and import more expensive ones.

Jim Wallis, editor of *Sojourners* magazine, dramatically indicates the effects of institutionalized injustice related to trade laws and other economic conditions:

We are finally coming to understand a discomforting but central fact of reality—the people of the non-industrialized world are poor *because* we are rich; the poverty and brutalization of the wretched masses is maintained and perpetuated by our systems and institutions and by the way we live our lives. In other words, the oppressive conditions of life in the poor countries, like the causes of poverty and misery in our own land, are neither merely accidental nor because of the failures of the poor. Our throwaway culture of affluence and wasteful consumption fragments and privatizes our lives. Our consumer orientation lulls us into primary concern for ourselves and into a passive acceptance of the suffering of others—horrors committed in our name in Indochina and elsewhere. At home, our consumerism supports corporate interests that exploit the poor, profit from war, and destroy the environment. Peace, justice, and ecological survival are sacrificed for the rewards and pleasures of affluence. Our present standard and style of life can be maintained or expanded only at the cost of the suppression of the poor of the world.[14]

In her poem, "Thank You, Tio Sam (Uncle Sam)," Mary Mackey relates that while many people in wealthy countries feel that their governments are helping the underdeveloped world, to Third-World people, "Gringo aid is a national disaster." She relates how we forced them to grow coffee instead of corn. The result was inevitably their children's starvation. Ms. Mackey also reports that we took their cattle and other meat and left them with nothing to eat.[15]

Unfortunately, the U.S. has been struggling against changes that are necessary for a more just and peaceful world. As Arnold Toynbee, the noted British historian, put it: "America is today the leader of a worldwide antirevolutionary movement in defense of vested interests."[16]

Most Americans will be shocked and distressed by this analysis. They look on the United States as the defender of democracy around the world. They see our country as the "breadbasket of the world," providing food and other resources to the world's needy. The idea that the U.S. has acted primarily in support of corporate interests regardless of negative effects on the majority of people in poorer countries is completely foreign to their thinking. But let us consider the statements of some Americans who have been actively involved in carrying out U.S. diplomatic and military policy to maintain our business dominance.

Maj. Gen. Smedley D. Butler described how he rose through the ranks in the Marine Corps ". . . being a high-class muscle man for Big Business, for Wall Street, and for the bankers, . . . a racketeer for capitalism."[17] He was rewarded with honors, medals, and promotion because he ". . . helped make Mexico and especially Tampico safe for American oil interests in 1914 . . . helped make Haiti and Cuba a decent place for the National City Bank boys to collect revenues in . . . helped purify Nicaragua for the international banking house of

Brown Brothers in 1909–1912 . . . helped make Honduras 'right' for American fruit companies in 1903. . . ."[18]

For a more recent analysis, consider these words of Ralph McGehee, who served in the CIA from 1952 to 1977:

> My view, backed by 25 years of experience is, quite simply that the CIA is the covert action arm of the presidency. Most of its money, manpower, and energy go into covert operations that . . . include backing dictators and overthrowing democratically elected governments. . . . The CIA uses ·disinformation, much of it aimed at the U.S. public to mold opinion. . . . The U.S. installs foreign leaders, arms their armies, and empowers their police to help those leaders repress an angry, defiant people. . . . The CIA-empowered leaders represent only a small fraction who kill, torture, and impoverish their own people to maintain their position of privilege.[19]

Our backing of corporate business interests continues today as we back an oppressive regime in El Salvador, in spite of widespread reports of its major human rights violations, and arm and train disaffected expatriates and former supporters of Somoza in attempts to overthrow the Sandinist Government of Nicaragua. By constantly backing oppressive governments and groups in Latin America, we often leave Latin Americans battling oppression no choice but to turn to Cuba and the Soviet Union, as the only available sources of help. Our present and past policies have led to much anti-U.S. feeling in Latin America and other parts of the world.

The previous discussions should not be taken as condoning brutal Soviet policies. Their lack of freedom, their anti-Semitism, their failure to permit Jews to emigrate, and their repressive internal and external policies must be sharply condemned. But Soviet policies should not be used as an excuse for the misdeeds of our own government. While we pride ourselves in being democratic, why do we back so many cruel, despotic regimes? Why is our tax money being used to supply the means of repression to dictatorships?[20] These comments and questions are based on the belief that the highest form of patriotism lies in challenging one's country to live up to its highest ideals.

The choice cannot be only between Soviet totalitarianism and authoritarian governments backed by the U.S. to support our perceived national and corporate interests. There is another way, a way that is necessary for global survival. This is the way of really applying Jewish values: *bal tashchit* (less waste), so that we are not dependent on repressive regimes for resources; "every person created in God's image," so we work to end violations of human rights, wherever they occur; the pursuit of justice—to end the conditions whereby a minority of the world's people prosper while the majority lack food and other basic human needs; the pursuit of peace, so that an insane arms race that drains the world's labor, ingenuity, and resources can be ended. Only these alternatives can result in global harmony and humane conditions for the world's people.

A New International Economic Order

Recently the underdeveloped countries have been calling for a New International Economic Order, in order to reduce the growing inequalities between the wealthy and poor countries. It includes at least five key elements[21]:

- meeting the basic human needs of all, before providing luxuries for a few;
- increasing people's opportunities to be involved in economic and political decision making, rather than having decisions made by a few rulers, a local elite, or corporations;
- promoting self-reliance strategies so that there is reduced dependence on foreign sources for food and other basic needs;
- development of a technology that builds on the culture, skills, and resources of each people and country, rather than importing technology that is more appropriate to industrialized countries; and
- protection of people's basic human rights and an end to oppressive rule of military dictatorships.

The underdeveloped countries' need for a New International Economic Order was eloquently stressed by Bishop J. D. Sangu of Tanzania to the forty-first International Eucharistic Conference held in Philadelphia in 1976:

> In international affairs and international trade the developing countries are still almost completely at the mercy of the developed countries.
> They dictate the world market, they fix tariffs and quotas, they determine the prices of raw materials and primary products. They establish the prices of the processed products, they determine the monetary system and control the circulation of money through the International Monetary Fund and the World Bank. . . .

112

And one of the basic principles of this world order is that as long as you make a profit for your own purse it does not matter that you plunder others. . . . The people of the Third World realize more and more now that the only means to save them from perennial poverty and hunger is the creation of a New International Economic Order, based on mutual agreement between all nations, aimed at equal justice for all, through equitable distribution of the world's riches and resources.[22]

In seeking a New International Economic Order, the poor countries are not asking for charity or even aid. They are seeking changes in the economic system so they can improve their economic conditions through their own efforts; they want a fair price for their raw materials, so they can afford manufactured goods and social services necessary for their development. They are attempting to negotiate as a group for better economic conditions for all countries, which will lead toward social, economic, and political peace.

Certainly the principles of the NIEO are consistent with Jewish values such as sharing global resources (which, in the final analysis, belong to God), justice, the brotherhood and equality of every person, and providing opportunities for people to become self-reliant.

In addition to a New International Economic Order, there is a need for new internal economic orders in many countries. Otherwise, rapid economic growth in a country will not mean better economic conditions for its people. For example, Brazil, under a military dictatorship strongly backed by the U.S., had economic growth at the rate of 10 percent annually from 1968–74. But, according to Brazil's minister of finance, only 5 percent of the people benefitted from the tremendous economic growth. The poorest two-thirds of Brazilians saw their real purchasing power decline by 50 percent from 1965 to 1974. Meanwhile, 40 percent of Brazil's 110 million people suffered from malnutrition.[23]

The *New York Times* reported that while Brazil's gross national product rose by 150 percent during twelve years of right-wing military rule, there was a sharp redistribution of income in favor of the wealthy.[24] They later reported that the rapid expansion of Brazil's agriculture was primarily for the well-to-do, the local elites.[25]

Brazil's increasing income gaps are indicated by the following: From 1960 to 1970, the share of income for the poorest 40 percent dropped from 10 to 8 percent, while the wealthiest 5 percent increased their share of total income from 29 to 38 percent.[26]

Most other Latin American countries and many countries in Asia and Africa have situations comparable to that in Brazil. In the developing countries, the richest 20 percent of the populations earn 51.4

percent of the national income, while the poorest 20 percent earn only 5.8 percent of the national income.[27] In Mexico, in 1977, the richest 20 percent earned 58 percent of the national income compared with only 3 percent earned by the poorest 20 percent.[28] In most poor countries, a relatively small local elite are doing very well economically, while the majority are barely surviving.

Considering these statistics, it is not too difficult to see why there have been many revolutions in recent years and why there is unrest in many countries today.

Let us consider Nicaragua, where a revolution has recently taken place. Nicaragua is a poor country experiencing rapid population growth. In 1979, when the revolution began, over 12 percent of its children died in their first year. It had a very high birth rate (47 births per 1,000 population) and a very young population (48 percent of the people under fifteen years of age), which means that its rapid population growth will be hard to slow down.[29] Nicaragua's population was projected to double in just twenty years[30]; at that rate there would be thirty-two Nicaraguans a century from now for every one today. The life expectancy in Nicaragua was relatively low, fifty-three years (twenty years less than in the U.S.); only 3 percent of the population was over sixty-four years of age (compared to a world average of 6 percent).[31] The Physical Quality of Life Index (an indication of conditions for the people in a country, based on measures of infant mortality, literacy, and life expectancy at one year of age) was only 55 (below the world average of 65).[32] Considering all of the above, it is not surprising that there was a revolution in Nicaragua.

Recently Frances Moore Lappé and Joseph Collins (authors of *Food First* and co-directors of the Institute for Food and Development Policy) took "a journey through the new Nicaragua," where they talked to a wide variety of Nicaraguans to assess the effects of the revolution. They concluded that while Nicaragua has many problems, people's lives have markedly improved in many aspects[33]:

- Expenditures for health and education have more than tripled, compared to even the best year under Somoza.
- Compared to 1977–78, production of basic foods is up: beans by 45 percent and rice by 100 percent.
- Using a volunteer-based literacy campaign, the illiteracy rate has been dramatically cut from over half of the population to less than one-seventh. Over 1,200 new schools have been built, primarily in the countryside.
- Almost 40,000 landless rural families have received access to land where they can grow food.

- While further progress is necessary, there is some freedom of speech, religion, association, and the press—greater than that found in many Latin American countries that the U.S. supports.

Although it is a repressive dictatorship, and despite unyielding antagonism from the United States, Cuba has also achieved advances for its people.[34] Life expectancy, which was fifty-five years in 1959, is now seventy-three years—on a par with developed countries; infant mortality has dropped steadily from 7 percent before the revolution to under 2 percent today; Cuba's literacy rate is over 95 percent, the highest in Latin America; expenditures on public health and education are over 20 percent of its national budget. Cuba's free public education system is the best in Latin America, with 92 percent of children under sixteen attending school.

Struggles in other oppressed Third World countries for more just internal orders have not been as successful, sometimes due to negative effects of the present international economic order. This led Michael Manley, former prime minister of Jamaica, to state:

> For all small Third World countries, their attempt to change themselves has to begin with the problem of changing the world. If you can't change the world, if you can't change the distribution of wealth in the world, you haven't a chance of changing, really, the condition of any of the small Third World parts of the world.[35]

Judaism and International Concerns

Judaism involves both particular and universal concerns. The particular aspects include observances related to the Sabbath and holy days, rules of *kashrut* (kosher food), and proper conduct during prayer. Jews are to be especially concerned about their co-religionists: "All Israel is responsible, one for another" (Shevuot 39a).

However, the message of Judaism is universal, expressing concern for every person and nation. We have already discussed many Jewish teachings related to humanity: Every person is created in God's image; every life is sacred and should be treated with dignity and respect; we should be kind to the stranger, for we were strangers in the land of Egypt; we should even show compassion to enemies. Other Jewish universal teachings are indicated below:

- The first covenant God made was with Noah, on behalf of the entire human race, and the animal kingdom (Genesis 9:11).

- As indicated previously, Abraham challenged God on behalf of the non-Hebrew cities of Sodom and Gemorah. To save the righteous, he pleaded, "Shall not the judge of all the earth do justly?" (Genesis 18:25).
- Some of the noblest characters in Scripture are not presented as Jewish. Ruth—a Moabite, who later became an Israelite—is presented as a model of an ideal human being, representing the values of kindness, self-sacrificing loyalty, and love. Job, the symbol of the righteous person who maintains his faith in God in spite of unprecedented suffering, is not presented as a Jew.
- Some of Israel's greatest leaders were descendants of proselytes. This includes King David, who is considered to be the ancestor of the Messiah. The Eighteen Benedictions of the Prayer Book include a special prayer for "righteous proselytes." Hillel, the foremost Talmudic sage of his day, received converts with special eagerness.
- Even of the traditional enemy of the Jew, the Edomites, it is said; "You shall not abhor an Edomite, for he is your brother" (Deuteronomy 23:8).
- The prophets stress that Jews have a universal mandate, a charge to improve conditions for all the world's people. Consider, for example, these words of Isaiah (Isaiah 42:6–7):

> Thus saith God, the Lord. . . .
> I the Lord have called thee in righteousness,
> And have taken hold of thy hand,
> And kept thee, and set thee for a covenant of the people,
> For a light unto the nations;
> To open the blind eyes,
> To bring the prisoners from the dungeon,
> And them that sit in darkness out of the prison house.

- Throughout their history, Jews have worked not for individual salvation, but for salvation for the entire world:

> In that day, there shall be a highway from Egypt to Assyria. The Assyrians shall join with the Egyptians and Egyptians with Assyrians, and both countries shall serve the Lord.
> In that day, Israel shall be a third partner with Egypt and Assyria as a blessing on earth; for the Lord of Hosts will bless them, saying, "Blessed be My people, Egypt, My handiwork Assyria, and my very own Israel."
>
> Isaiah 19:23–25

- Hillel, in his famous formulation, teaches that we must be concerned with other people as well as ourselves:

  > If I am not for myself, who will be for me?
  > But if I am only for myself, what am I?
  > And if not now, when?
  > Pirke Avot 1:14

- The prophet Malachi (2:10) powerfully expressed Jewish universal concerns:

  > Have we not all one father?
  > Hath not one God created us?
  > Why then do we deal treacherously with one another, profaning the covenant of our fathers?

- Amos (9:7) proclaims God's concern for all nations:

  > Are you not like the Ethiopians to Me, O people of Israel?
  > says the Lord,
  > Did I not bring up Israel from the land of Egypt,
  > and the Philistines from Caphtor; and the Syrians from Kir?

- Jeremiah was appointed as "a prophet to the nations" (Jeremiah 1:5). He was told (1:10):

  > See, I have set you this day over nations and over Kingdoms,
  > To pluck up and to break down,
  > To destroy and to overthrow,
  > To build and to plant.

- The Book of Jonah shows God's concern for the people of Nineveh, the very people who destroyed the ancient state of Israel. Jonah, a Jew, is sent to teach the people of Nineveh to serve God, and is taught that God cares for all people, and even animals.
- The Talmud states: "The pious of all nations shall have a place in the world to come."
- During the holiday of Sukkot in the days of the Temple of Jerusalem, seventy sacrifices were made for the "seventy nations" (the Hebrew expression in those days for all of humanity).

    The *sukkah* (temporary abode of the Jew during Sukkot) must possess enough of an opening on the top so that the Jew can see the universe outside and be reminded that there are peoples and nations outside his or her own, which must be considered.

The palm branch (lulav) used during Sukkot is waved to the north, south, east, and west after a benediction is recited, to signify that God's sovereignty is universal and that when we pray for salvation and help, we must think of these blessings not only for ourselves, but for humanity.

Rabbi Haninah felt that salvation for the world could come only when the nations accepted the lesson of the sukkah and the lulav: that no nation can enjoy happiness unless there is harmony among all nations.[36]

●. The sages declare that the Torah can be accepted by any person:

> The Torah was given in public, openly, in a free place. For had the Torah been given in the land of Israel, the Israelites could have said to the nations of the world: "You have no share in it." But now that it was given in the wilderness publicly and openly in a place that is free for all, everyone willing to accept it could come and accept it.
>
> Mechilta D'Rabbi Ishmael

● A chassidic Midrash beautifully expresses the universal spirit of Judaism:

> "Why," the student asked, "is the stork called Chasidah, the loving one?"
>
> "Because," the rabbi answered, "he gives so much love to his mate and to his young."
>
> "Then why," asked the student, "if he gives so much love to his mate and to his young, is the stork considered trefe (forbidden) rather than kosher?"
>
> "He is considered trefe," the rabbi answered, "because he gives love only to his own."[37]

The concept of Jews as a "chosen" people has often been misinterpreted. The prophets remind the people that chosenness does not mean divine favoritism or immunity from punishment; on the contrary, it means being more seriously exposed to God's judgment and chastisement:

Hear this word that the Lord has spoken against you, O people of Israel, against the whole family which I brought up out of the land of Egypt: You only have I known of all the families of the earth; Therefore I will punish you for all your iniquities.

Amos 3:1–2

"Chosenness" does not mean that God is exclusively concerned with Israel. As Jewish history attests, it certainly does not mean that Jews will prosper and be free of troubles.

Judaism's international vision is one of peace and righteousness for humanity:

In the end of days it shall come to pass,
That the mountain of the Lord's house shall be established on
    the top of the mountains,
And it shall be exalted above the hills.
Peoples shall flow unto it,
And many nations shall come and say,
"Come, let us go up to the mountain of the Lord,
To the house of the God of Jacob;
So that He may teach us of His ways,
And we will walk in His paths;
For the law shall go forth from Zion,
And the word of the Lord from Jerusalem."
And He shall judge among many peoples,
And rebuke strong nations afar off;
They shall beat their swords into plowshares
And their spears into pruning-hooks;
Nation shall not lift up sword against nation;
Neither shall they learn war anymore.
They shall sit every man under his vine and under his fig-tree;
And none shall make them afraid;
For the mouth of the Lord of hosts has spoken it.
For as all the peoples walk every one in the name of his god,
We will walk in the name of the Lord our God forever.

Micah 4:1–5

For global harmony, "a law (Torah) must go out of Zion." Such a "law" has been proclaimed, but the nations have refused to acknowledge it. It is a law that states that there is one Creator of the entire world, that every person, created in God's image, of infinite worth, must be able to share in the bounties provided by God's earth, and that people and nations must seek and pursue peace, pursue justice, and love others, since they are like themselves. If people and nations took seriously this law out of Zion, there would be harmony, peace, and sufficient resources for all the world's people.

Micah's words provide a moral covenant for the world, a covenant rooted in truth and justice that supports the structure of peace. This is explicitly spelled out by the following Talmudic teaching:

Upon three things the world rests, upon justice, upon truth, and upon peace. And the three are one, for when justice is done, truth prevails, and peace is established.

Ta'anit 4:2; Megilla 3:5

While the prophets believed that nations would continue, they looked forward to the moralization of national loyalities. They were true internationalists who urged the creation of proper relations among nations, based on peace, justice, and truth. Their vision represented a farsighted interpretation of nationalism, in which love of one's country and loyalty to humanity represent two concentric circles.[38] The philospher Santayana stated, "A man's feet may be firmly planted in his own country, but his eyes survey the world." Rabbi Robert Gordis added: "The prophets went further, their hearts embraced the world. . . ."[39]

Consistent with Jewish tradition and values, Jews must be in the forefront of those working for a New International Economic Order and new internal economic orders, so that nations will finally be able to beat their swords into plowshares and each person will be able to sit, unafraid, "under his vine and fig-tree."

Chapter 11

Energy

A generation goes and a generation comes but the earth
endures forever.
And the sun rises and the sun sets—then to its place it rushes;
there it rises again. It goes toward the south and veers
toward the north.
The wind goes round and round, and on its rounds the wind
returns.
All the rivers flow into the sea, yet the sea is not full; to the
place where the rivers flow, there they flow once more.
                                         —Ecclesiastes 1:4–7

The United States and the rest of the world are suffering in many ways because of inadequate energy policies. Our very wasteful use of energy has made the U.S. dependent on other countries for much of its fuel supply. This has hampered our foreign policy options, especially in the volatile Middle East. It has also contributed to record balance of payments deficits and many other economic problems, such as budget deficits and unemployment. Extensive burning of fossil fuels has resulted in many present and potential environmental problems including oil spills, air pollution, acid rain, and possible climate changes.[1]

Energy experts generally agree that our present reliance on oil and natural gas must end in the near future. After decades of growth, U.S. oil production peaked in 1970 and has declined every year since. World oil production is expected to have a similar downturn within ten years.[2] While there has been an "oil glut" recently, largely due to a worldwide recession, energy researchers generally agree that the era of cheap, readily available fossil fuels is ending and new energy policies are necessary.

The two major energy options can be characterized, in the words of energy expert Amory Lovins, as the "hard" path and the "soft" path.[3] The hard path assumes that we can obtain sufficient energy from coal, uranium, and synthetic sources to continue our historic increase in energy use and that, in fact, such increased energy consumption is necessary for our country to prosper. Advocates of the soft path feel that energy efficiency and conservation are prime answers to current problems and that renewable energy sources based on sun, wind, flowing water, and biomass should be used to eliminate dangers associated with hard energy fuels.

What criteria should be used to select a proper energy path? Certainly they should include such Jewish values as *bal tashchit* (thou shall not waste), "the earth is the Lord's," the sanctity of every life, consideration for future generations, dignity of labor, and proper use of God's cycles of sun, wind, and water. Let us consider energy choices with respect to each of these principles.

Bal Tashchit

Consistent with the biblical mandate not to waste or unnecessarily destroy anything of value (Deuteronomy 20:19,20), the heart of the soft energy path is strong reliance on conservation.

The U.S. is extremely wasteful of energy. With only 5 percent of the world's people, we use about 35 percent of its energy and resources.[4] According to energy expert Denis Hayes, we waste about half of the energy that we use; this wasted energy equals the energy used by two-thirds of the world's people. Several countries, such as Sweden, Switzerland, and West Germany, use 60 percent as much energy per person as we do, while having standards of living comparable to ours.[5] Due to wasteful energy use, U.S. electrical energy demand has doubled every ten years for most of the twentieth century.

Energy derived from conservation is cheaper, safer, more reliable, less polluting, and more job-creating than energy obtained from any other source.[6] Conservation doesn't mean, as President Reagan recently put it, being "too hot in the summer and too cold in the winter." It does mean more effective use of the fuel we use: more-efficient automobiles, better-insulated homes and offices, reuse of resources, gadgets and machines designed for longer life, and lights and equipment turned off when not being used.

Several recent studies have shown that we can continue to grow and maintain and improve our life-styles while reducing our use of energy. In a 1979 report, "The Good News about Energy," the U.S. Council on Environmental Quality stated that the U.S. economy can operate on 30 to 40 percent less energy without a reduction in growth.[7] The National Academy of Sciences concluded that by the year 2010, we could reduce energy use by 20 percent while sustaining continued energy and population growth. Similar conclusions were given in reports by the Harvard Business School[8] and CBS news.

The American Economic Association stated in 1977: "By 2000, energy consumption can be reduced by 9 percent below current levels, while GNP increases by 80 percent."

In an ad in the *New York Times* in 1980, Union Carbide Corporation stated: "Some experts believe Americans could live as comfortably on 30 to 40 percent less energy if conservation became a way of life." They also pointed out: "The economic advantages of improving energy efficiency are compelling. . . . A $15,000 investment to conserve one barrel (of oil) every day, for example, pays for itself in about two years at today's oil prices." They called for new governmental financial incentives to make America more energy efficient.

Many corporations and individuals have sharply reduced their energy consumption in recent years. The Port Authority of New York, for example, announced in February 1981 that it had reduced its energy use by 50 percent and its fuel oil consumption by 80 percent since 1973.[9] Through operational and equipment changes, use of advanced technology, and better control of building temperatures and lighting, the Port Authority saved $105 million from 1973 to 1981. This conserved energy could supply all the electrical, heating, air conditioning, and lighting needs of New York's World Trade Center for 2½ years.

"The Earth Is the Lord's and the Fullness Thereof" (Psalms 24:1)

Soft energy methods based on renewable resources and conservation have relatively minor effects on the environment. The hard energy path, on the other hand, entails many current and potential threats to ecosystems[10]:

- Effluents from coal-burning power plants, such as sulfur dioxide and particulate matter (particles), pollute the air. Especially when acting together, these pollutants have very detrimental effects on health.
- When high smokestacks are used, sulfur dioxide from coal-burning power plants combines with water vapor and forms sulfuric acid. Later this falls to the earth as acid rain, which has badly damaged many crop areas and lakes in Canada and the Adirondack Mountains.
- Major oil spills, such as the recent ones in Santa Barbara and

the Gulf of Mexico, severely damage marine life.

- Heated waters ejected from power-plant cooling systems cause thermal pollution, which affects the delicate balance in ecological systems of lakes, rivers, and oceans.
- Surface strip mining for coal destroys land and results in acids running off and polluting nearby waters.

The Sanctity of Life

Soft energy methods involve minimal or no danger to human life. The hard energy path, in contrast, endangers life in several ways:

- In spite of numerous health and safety advances in the last ten years, underground coal mining is still the most dangerous job. On the average, one worker dies in the coal industry every two working days; a coal miner is eight times more likely to die on the job than an average private sector worker.[11] Every year, sixty-three of every thousand coal miners are disabled by injuries.[12] Many more suffer the painful and debilitating disease of "black lung," which often results in death.[13]
- Air pollution from fossil-fuel power plants often leads to disease and death.
- Nuclear power plants pose great potential threats to life. Nuclear facilities expose workers and surrounding communities to cumulative doses of low-level radiation, which many scientists believe can result in various kinds of cancer, as well as genetic damage that may be passed on to future generations.
- It was estimated that by 1974 more than 230 uranium miners' deaths were related to exposure to radiation.[14]

Consideration for Future Generations

Judaism stresses that we must consider the effects of our activities on future generations. A Talmudic sage posed the question "Who is the wise person?" His response: "The person who foresees the future consequences of his actions."

The Talmud tells a story of a very old man who was planting a carob tree, which would not bear fruit for many years. When asked why he was planting it, he explained that just as he had been able to partake of the fruits of trees others had planted many years ago, he also wanted to plant for those who would come after him (Ta'anit 23a; Leviticus Rabbah 25:5).

Soft energy methods do not have potential negative effects for future generations. Conservation is actually an investment in the future, since saved energy and resources can meet the needs of our descendants. Use of renewable sources such as sun, wind, and water does not lead to future scarcities, which could result in inflation and potential conflicts.

Once again, hard energy sources come out second best. Among potential negative effects for future generations are the following:

- Three decades after the U.S. atomic electric power industry began accumulating nuclear waste, with temporary repositories quickly filling up, there is no safe, practical method of storing radioactive waste material. Radioactive wastes are toxic, and once released into the environment, would contaminate land and water virtually "forever."
- A nuclear accident could release enough radiation to kill thousands of people and contaminate cities, land, and water for decades. Heavily populated areas near nuclear power plants are finding it difficult to plan an adequate evacuation.
- Nuclear waste products can be used by nations or terrorist groups to make nuclear weapons. It is expected that within a decade, over thirty nations, many with unstable governments, will have the capacity to explode an atomic warhead.
- The many potential dangers related to nuclear power were summarized by Nobel Prize-winning physicist Hannes Alfven:
  Fission energy is safe only if a number of critical devices work as they should, if a number of people in key positions follow all of their instructions, if there is no sabotage, no hijacking of transports, if no reactor fuel processing plant or waste repository anywhere in the world is situated in a region of riots or guerrilla activity, and no revolution or war—even a "conventional" one—takes place in these regions. . . . No acts of God can be permitted.[15]
- Guarding nuclear facilities raises threats to our civil liberties as well. In a document prepared for the Nuclear Regulatory Commission in 1975, a Stanford University law professor stated that, in light of potential nuclear-related theft and terrorism, there might be a need for "a nationwide guard force, greater surveillance of dissenting political groups, area searches in the event of loss of material, and creation of new barriers of secrecy. . . ."[16] He also anticipated wiretapping, detention, and

harsh interrogation, perhaps even involving torture.

- As indicated before, the carbon dioxide buildup in the atmosphere due to fossil-fuel burning may cause a "greenhouse effect," which can change climate, with negative effects on agriculture and possible flooding of large coastal areas.

The Dignity of Labor

Unlike many ancient societies, such as those of Greece and Rome, where manual labor was despised and physical work was done by slaves, Judaism stresses the dignity of creative labor. Work is considered a character-developing process that gives an individual self-respect and respect from others.

Many Jewish teachings stress its great esteem for creative labor.[17]

A man should love work, and no man should hate work. For even as the sabbath was commanded to the Jews as a covenant at Sinai, so was labor enjoined in that covenant, as it is said, "Six days shalt thou labor and do all thy work" (and only then it is written), "the seventh day is a sabbath unto the Lord thy God" (Exodus 20:9,10).

Avot de Rabbi Nathan 11:23a

When a man eats of his own labors, his mind is at ease, but when a man eats of the labors of his father or mother or children, his mind is not at ease, and how much more so when he has to eat of the labors of strangers.

Avot de Rabbi Nathan 31

Soft energy methods are labor-intensive. Many jobs can be created in such areas as weatherization of homes to make them more energy efficient, recycling of products, and construction of equipment for production and distribution of renewable energy. According to a study prepared for the Energy Subcommittee of the Congressional Joint Economic Committee, the U.S. can gain 3 million jobs by 1990 by adopting an energy policy based on solar energy and conservation.[18]

By contrast, hard energy paths are capital intensive. They require sophisticated, expensive equipment, but relatively few workers.

Proper Use of God's Cycles of Sun, Wind, and Water

A major cause of pollution and resource shortage problems in recent years is that we have been misusing God's cycles of sun, earth, wind, and water due to greed and faulty technology.

Use of fossil fuels to create energy causes pollution and depletes finite resources, which increases the difficulty and expense of getting future energy. Usage of soft energy sources prevents these problems.

Hence, in partnership with conservation, the second major part of the soft energy path is use of renewable fuels based on sun, wind, and water. Denis Hayes pointed out that, if political obstacles can be overcome, such sources can provide 40 percent of global energy requirements by the year 2000 and 75 percent by 2025.[19] At the present time, solar energy is expensive, but increased research and greater use would lower the cost of individual units.

Israel is a world leader in developing solar energy equipment. Visitors are generally impressed by the many solar water heaters on the roofs of apartment buildings. Solar energy systems are being rapidly developed in Israel since sunlight is its most abundant energy source.

There are many "hidden" benefits of solar sources: They are generally pollution-free, renewable, dependable, abundant, decentralized, safe, job-creating, and inflation-resistant.

These factors should be contrasted with the many "hidden costs" of hard energy sources: air and water pollution, negative health effects, the need for giant cooling towers, possible major changes in our climate, nuclear wastes that must be stored for thousands of years, record balance of payment deficits, a foreign policy hampered by our dependence on other countries for fuel, possible extensive blackouts, and potential blackmail from terrorist groups that can gain the means of producing nuclear weapons.

In summary, our nation can best be served by an energy policy based on Jewish values that emphasize CARE (Conservation And Renewable Energy).[20] Such a policy means turning away from sources of energy which have become environmentally unacceptable and extremely costly; simpler technology and less reliance on central electrical generating plants; less dependence on large energy companies and Arab and other foreign governments, which can cut off supplies or sharply raise prices; a simpler world, with more conservation of energy and resources; a safer world, with less competition for scarce fuels and other commodities; a more stable economy; less unemployment; and more money available for education, health, housing, transportation, nutrition, and social services. The Jewish community must lead the call for energy policies that will lead to this safer, saner future.

Chapter 12

Population Growth

For the Jewish people, the problem [of the population bomb] does not exist. On the contrary, it would be more accurate to describe our situation as a "Population Bust"... which spells demographic disaster for Jewry.[1]

You can't say that the world suffers from over-population and at the same time say Jews should ignore this. I don't want to put myself in the vulnerable position of saying it's good for the Puerto Ricans and poor South Americans to cut back on their population and not the Jews. I've never thought for a moment that the way you insure Jewish viability is sheer weight of numbers.[2]

These quotations epitomize the apparent dilemma facing Jews today. While world population grows rapidly, with many negative results, there has been great concern about the effects of *reduced* Jewish population and assimilation. Before considering what a proper Jewish response to this issue might be, let us consider the nature of the population problem, and Jewish teachings regarding procreation.

One of the critical problems the world faces today is that of explosive population growth. There is widespread concern about the world's ability to provide enough food, energy, housing, employment, education, and health care for the world's increasing population while simultaneously protecting our environment, quality of life, and political freedom.

Population statistics are staggering.[3] While it took all of human history for the world's population to reach 1 billion people, the population now increases at the rate of 1 billion every ten to twelve years. Global population reached four billion in 1976 and is expected to top 6 billion by the end of the century. Every three years the world's increase is greater than the population of the U.S., and every six months, the increase equals the amount of people killed in all the world's wars in the last 500 years.

At current rates, the world's population will double to over 9 billion people in approximately forty years.[4] Many poor countries, such as Honduras and Nicaragua, have population-doubling periods of only twenty years.[5] This means that, in order to maintain present, generally inadequate conditions, these countries must double their supply of food, energy, clean water, housing, schools, and jobs in twenty years. For many countries, this may prove impossible; the result may be increasing poverty, malnutrition, civil unrest, and revolution.

Additional population problems are related to the increasing movement of people from rural areas to cities, searching for better jobs and social conditions. Mexico City had three million people in 1950; over 30 million are projected by the year 2000.[6] The population of Lima, Peru, grew by over 1,600 percent in a recent fifty-year period.[7] Such Third World cities have been unable to meet the needs of their rapidly growing populations. Slums have formed on the outskirts of the cities, with inadequate housing, sanitation, employment, and education and great potential for social unrest.

While there has been some recent progress in slowing the rate of population increase, the following factors contribute to population growth momentum:

- Birth rates have actually dropped recently in most countries of the world, but death rates have decreased even more sharply due to better medical and sanitary conditions, and are likely to continue to decline.
- The largest population increases are occurring in poor countries, where children are desired for economic reasons.[8] Due to increasing inflation and unemployment, the absolute number of destitute people is increasing.
- Forty percent of people in poorer countries are under fifteen years of age.[9] Thus many people will soon be moving into their reproductive years.

Many people feel rapid population growth is the greatest problem the world faces and that too many people in the world result in hunger, resource depletion, and environmental degradation. They advocate ZPG, zero population growth. A group with this title[10] has been working to educate people to problems related to population and the need to reduce U.S. births and rate of immigration. They encourage couples to voluntarily limit their reproduction to a maximum of two children. They believe that only with a stabilized population will the world's inhabitants be able to have clean air and water, a decent place to live, a meaningful job, good education, and treatment as individuals, rather than statistics. Another group, Negative Population Growth, argues that we have already passed the optimum U.S. population and we must eventually decrease our population.[11]

Based on Jewish tradition, how should Jews respond to arguments of advocates of reduced family size? The first *mitzvah* of the Torah is the duty of procreation. On the sixth day of creation, God created human beings (male and female), and He blessed them and said unto them:

> Be fruitful and multiply, and replenish the earth, and subdue it; and have dominion over the fish of the sea and over the fowl of the air, and over every living thing that moves upon the earth.
>
> Genesis 1:28

Later, after the Flood, this blessing was repeated to Noah: "Be fruitful and multiply, and replenish the earth" (Genesis 9:1).

The blessing of fertility was extended to Abraham and Sarah (Genesis 17:16). Through Isaac, Abraham was to be blessed with seed as numerous as the stars of heaven and as the sand on the seashore (Genesis 15:5). This blessing was repeated to Jacob, in the early years of his life (Genesis 28:14, 32:12) and also later (Genesis 35:11). The chief blessing that biblical personalities conferred on their children and grandchildren related to fertility. This was true of Isaac's blessing to Jacob (Genesis 28:3), Jacob's blessing to Manasseh and Ephraim (his grandchildren) (Genesis 48:16), and Jacob's blessing to Joseph (Genesis 49:25).

The following is one of many Talmudic passages that stress the importance of having children:

> Rabbi Eliezer stated: "He who does not engage in the propagation of the race is as though he sheds blood; for it is said, 'whoso sheddeth man's blood, by man shall his blood be shed,' and this is immediately followed by the text, 'And you, be ye fruitful and multiply.'" Rabbi Jacob said: "(One who does not propagate), it is as though he has diminished the Divine image; since it is said, 'For in the image of God made He man,' and this is immediately followed by, 'And you be fruitful.'" Ben Azzai said: "It is as though he sheds blood *and* diminishes the Divine image, since it is said, 'And you, be ye fruitful and multiply.'"[12]

Every human life is sacred and every new life brings God's image anew into the world. Hence Judaism has always regarded marriage and procreation as sacred duties and divine imperatives. People are to help populate the earth, for the world that God created is "very good" and people should follow God's commandment to be fruitful and multiply "with the intention of preserving the human species" (Maimonides, *Sefer Hamitzvot,* 212).

Judaism was never content with general formulations. Specific indications of how commandments were to be carried out were always given. Hence the Mishnah considered the question of how large a family one needed to satisfy the injunction to have children:

> A man shall not abstain from the performance of the duty of propagation of the race unless he already has children. As to the number, Bet Shammai (the school of Shammai) ruled: two males, and Bet Hillel ruled: a male and female, for it is stated in scripture, male and female created He them.
>
> Yebamot 61b

According to the Talmud, for Bet Shammai, the example for the sufficiency of two sons was Moses, who had two sons (Yebamot 61b). The disciples of Hillel base their opinion on the story of creation (Adam and Eve). The prevailing halachic opinion agrees with Bet Hillel.

Although the rabbis considered it meritorious for Jews to have large families, they looked at birth control more favorably after a couple had a son and a daughter.[13] However, generally rabbis encouraged couples not to follow the "*zwie kinder* (two children) system." This is consistent with Maimonides' injunction:

> Even if a person has fulfilled the commandment of "be fruitful and multiply," he is still enjoined not to refrain from fruitfulness and increase as long as he is able, for he who adds a life in Israel is as he who created a world.
>
> Mishneh Torah, Hilchot Ishut, 15:16

In spite of Judaism's strong emphasis on procreation, Jewish birth rates have declined sharply in recent years. Analysts agree that Jewish couples are not replacing themselves; the average number of children per Jewish family is about 1.7,[14] well below the replacement level of 2.1. Some population specialists argue that at current birth-and-death rates, the American Jewish population of 6 million will shrink to 4 million within seventy years.[15] Increasing trends toward single living, single-parent families, and the increasing age at marriage are expected to continue to depress Jewish birth rates.

Probably the most detailed study of recent Jewish population statistics is *Studies in Jewish Demography—Survey for 1972–1980,* a combined effort of the Institute of Contemporary Jewry at Hebrew University and the Institute of Jewish Affairs in London. The survey estimated that the Jewish population in the diaspora will fall by 20 to 25 percent from 10 million in 1975 to between 7.4 and 8.2 million by the year 2000. The number of Jews in Israel is projected to grow from under 3 million in 1975 to 4.4 to 4.7 million by the end of the century. Hence the total Jewish population, estimated at close to 13 million in 1975, is expected to decline to between 11.8 and 12.9 million by 2000. It should be noted that this decrease would occur at a time when world population is projected to *grow* from 4 billion to 6 billion people; hence there would be a sharp decline in the relative Jewish population.

Recent dramatic societal changes related to the Jewish family pose threats to the Jewish community[16]:

- One out of every two Jews who marry in the 1980s will be divorced by 1990.
- One out of every three Jewish college students who marry in the 1980s will marry a non-Jew.
- One out of every five married Jewish couples will have no Jewish children.
- One out of every two Jewish families will not be affiliated with a synagogue or any Jewish organization.
- Two out of every five Jewish children will receive no Jewish education and will not have a Bar or Bat Mitzvah.
- Approximately 40 percent of young adults in missionary and cult groups will be Jewish by birth.

Because of these facts, many Jews believe that one of the critical issues today is the question of Jewish survival. They see that the low Jewish birth rate, along with high rates of intermarriage and assimilation, poses a great danger to the Jewish people.

This is the central thesis of a new reference work: *Jewish Population: Renascence or Oblivion,* edited by Judith Zimmerman and Barbara Trainin, a record of the proceedings of a conference on Jewish population in 1978, sponsored by the Commission on Synagogue Relations of the Federation of Jewish Philanthropies. In her introduction, Judith Zimmerman, chairperson of the task force on Jewish population, indicated the twofold purpose of the conference:

(1) to sound an alarm and alert the Jewish community that: our Jewish population is declining. We are practicing negative pop-

ulation growth, i.e., we are not even replacing our present numbers. This phenomenon, coupled with increased assimilation and mixed marriages, threatens Jewish survival.

(2) To determine whether the Jewish community can, in the words of Dr. Steven Cohen (who presented a paper at the conference), "effectively intervene to minimize population losses."[17]

A July 14, 1975, *Time* magazine article, "The Disappearing Jews," stated that Orthodox rabbi Norman Lamm—now president of Yeshiva University—recommended that "each Jewish couple should have four or five children because Jews are a disappearing species." More recently, Rabbi Lamm called for immediate "bold and courageous action" by Jewish educators and community leaders to reverse a situation that "borders on the catastrophic."[18] He suggested steps to increase the Jewish birth rate, such as local federations providing scholarship money to large Jewish families, and instructing our children as young as nursery-school age in the concept that large families are the norm.

In June 1977, the Reform Movement's Central Conference of American Rabbis, a group that generally takes liberal stands, urged Jewish couples "to have at least two or three children."[19] In 1974, Rabbi Sol Roth, newly elected president of the New York Board of Rabbis, stated that "Jewish families should have at least three children, and the goal of zero population growth should find no application in the Jewish community."[20]

Jews have answered arguments of advocates of zero population growth in many ways.

- Since Jews constitute less than one-tenth of 1 percent of the world's population, the Jewish contribution to world population growth cannot matter significantly.
- Since 6 million Jews—one-third of the Jewish people—were killed in the Holocaust, Jews have a special obligation to bring children into the world to replace our numbers.
- Jews have made special contributions to the world, far beyond our very small proportion of the world's population, in many areas, such as science, the arts, education, business, and politics. Hence having more Jewish children would increase the general level of accomplishment in the world. It is also important that Judaism survive because the world badly needs the Jewish messages of peace, justice, and righteousness.

Rabbi David M. Feldman argues that "Jews have the paradoxical right to work for the cause of population control while regarding themselves as an exception to the rule."[21] To the response that other minorities will claim the same right, he argues that groups seeking to maintain a minority status and not to advance with respect to other groups should not be denied that right.

Some Jewish population activists have attacked the premises of the zero population growth movement. There is much merit in their argument, since, as discussed below, rapid population growth is not the prime cause of world problems. But they have generally ignored the facts that millions are dying annually due to hunger and its effects, half the world's people suffer from poverty, illiteracy, malnutrition, and disease, and the world's ecosystems are being increasingly threatened, to name just a few critical problems. They have also put great faith in technology as a solution to global problems, not taking into account that many of today's problems have been caused or worsened by the misuse of technology for many years.

Not all Jews agree that the Jewish community should urge couples to have larger families. In a recent article, "Population Panic—Why Jewish Leaders Want Jewish Women to be Fruitful and Multiply," Shirley Frank suggests that the "current panic" about Jewish fertility is an attack on the recent emergence of Jewish feminism.[22] She states that "additional childbearing and childrearing are likely to be at the expense of women's emergence and fulfillment, precisely at a time when . . . Jewish women are beginning to assert rightful claims for a life and an identity of their own, apart from their roles as wives and mothers."[23] She claims that virtually all the writers and speakers urging Jews to have more babies are male. She stresses that since birth rate is only one of the factors affecting Jewish survival, Jewish women can enhance the chances of Jewish survival in many ways other than having many children.

In an article in *Sh'ma* magazine (February 16, 1979), "We Need Quality More than Quantity," Paula E. Hyman argues that "the campaign for Jewish survival can be waged on many fronts" and Jewish women can contribute in many ways other than bearing children through their individual and various talents.

It should be pointed out that not all the indicators related to Jewish survival and health are negative[24]:

- Some segments of Judaism, such as the Traditional Orthodox and Chassidim, are growing in numbers; they tend to have high fertility, little or no intermarriage, and relatively little assimilation or apostasy from Judaism. The fact that these groups are often excluded partly or fully from surveys throws some doubt on the Jewish population trends previously discussed. These groups may be replenishing Jewish population, matching losses suffered by the larger, more modern population. This possibility is supported by the fact that in Israel, 10 percent of the families produce 40 percent of the children.[25]

- There has been a tremendous increase in the number of Jewish day schools. In the U.S., there are now about 400 under Orthodox administration and about 100 run by the Conservative and Reform movements. The nearly fifty Yeshivot for high school and college students gives the U.S. potential as a new center of Talmudic learning.

- There are many *ba'aley* and *ba'alot teshuvah* (returners to Orthodox Jewish observance) in the U.S., Israel, and the rest of the world. These people generally bring renewed dedication and involvement to Judaism.

- There have been several indications of renewed Jewish commitment among Reform Jews. New Reform prayerbooks contain more Hebrew and use of traditional terms such as *mitzvot*.In recent decades, the Reform movement has affirmed Jewish peoplehood, encouraged *aliyah,* and asserted that Jews have a stake and responsibility in building the state of Israel.

- While in 1970, Jewish programs on college campuses were very rare, by 1979, 337 colleges offered some Jewish courses, with 130 of them offering a major and/or a graduate degree in Jewish studies.[26] Hence many Jews are having serious encounters with Judaism on college campuses.

- Thousands of scholars are researching *Yiddishkeit* (Jewish tradition). Hebrew literature and Jewish scholarship are flourishing in Israel.

Hence in many ways, as a counter to the assimilation of many Jews, in the last generation there has been a marked improvement in the quality and intensity of Jewish life.

It should be pointed out that there have been many false prophecies of Jewish disappearance in the past. The late Professor Simon Rawidowicz pointed out, Jews are "the ever-dying people," each generation since early in Jewish history perceiving that it was the last one.[27] It is interesting to note that both Abraham and Isaac had two children and in each case 50 percent assimilated.

There are justifications in the Jewish tradition for considering the zero population growth philosophy:

- While in Egypt, Joseph had two sons during the seven years of plenty, but no additional children during the seven years of famine. The Biblical commentator Rashi interprets this to mean that when there is widespread hunger, one should not bring additional children into the world.[28]

- When he entered the ark, Noah was commanded to desist from procreation. The ark contained enough provisions only for those in the ark; to increase that number by reproduction would have upset its "ecology." Hence it might be concluded that it would be wrong to bring more children into the world if there is insufficient food for those already here.

- It could be argued that when Adam and later Noah were commanded to "be fruitful and multiply," the earth was far emptier than it is today. Now that the earth is "overfilled," as measured by the poverty, malnutrition, and squalor faced by so many of the world's people, the commandment may no longer apply.

There would thus seem to be some rationale for Jews to practice and advocate zero population growth (ZPG). But perhaps we should look more deeply into the problem. Are current crises due to too many people, or are there other, more important causes?

Perhaps what the world really needs is not ZPG, but ZPIG, zero population-impact growth. For it is not just the number of people that is important, but how much they produce, consume, and waste. Affluent nations have an effect on the environment disproportionate to their populations. The U.S., for example, has only 5 percent of the world's population, yet uses about 35 percent of the world's resources and energy, while producing half the world's pollution. It has been estimated that an average person in the U.S. has an impact on the world's life-support systems (in terms of resources consumed and pollution caused) equal to that of about fifty people in an underdeveloped country. This gives the U.S. a population impact equal to over 11 billion Third World people, well over twice the world's population.

At international population conferences, when delegates from affluent countries ask representatives from poor countries why they don't slow their population growth, they generally respond, "Why don't you stop being so wasteful? Why don't you stop using so much of the resources that we need to develop our countries so that our people will have the economic security necessary for them to consider having smaller families?"

Another important factor, often overlooked by advocates of population as that prime cause of global problems, is the unjust and inequitable systems that lead to poverty and malnutrition. Several studies have shown that the world now produces enough food to provide an adequate diet for every person on earth. Yet valuable land in poor countries is used to grow luxury crops for rich local elites or for export, while masses of people lack an adequate diet. Due to inequitable control over agricultural resources, only about half of the world's potential agricultural land is now being cultivated. In Ecuador, for example, only 14 percent of the tillable land is being used.[29] Trade laws are rigged against poor countries, keeping them on a perpetual treadmill; poor people constantly fall further behind, no matter how hard they work.

Why do people in the poorer countries have many children? For millions of people, there is no unemployment pay, sick leave, or old-age pension. Children, therefore, are regarded as the only form of security in periods of unemployment, illness, and old age. They are also an economic asset, because by the age of seven or eight, children are net contributors to the family—fetching water and firewood from distant places, looking after younger children, freeing adults for other jobs by cooking, cleaning, and mending clothes. Furthermore, infant mortality rates are still high in the underdeveloped world, and many children are desired so that some will survive to provide old-age security.

Because of these conditions, family planning programs, by themselves, are ineffective in lowering birth rates. It is necessary to improve the economic and social conditions so children are not depended on for economic survival and old-age security. It is significant that in the U.S. in the early 1800s, when infant mortality was high and help was needed on farms, the average couple had an average of eight children.

There are two prevalent attitudes about current population growth that can block steps necessary for global survival. One is that population is the greatest threat to the planet and must be combated via better birth control and family planning methods. This ignores the fact that population growth is a symptom and result of a wasteful, unjust world, and major changes in social, political, and economic systems are necessary to reduce population growth and other global threats.

The other dangerous attitude is that population growth is not a problem, that through technology we can provide enough food and other resources for all the world's people. This ignores the geometric (ever-doubling) nature of population growth and the fact that technology placed in an unjust, materialistic world has generally been part of the problem rather than part of the solution.

Population growth is not a root cause of global problems. With more just, equitable, and less wasteful systems, we could have enough food and other resources for all the world's current and future people. Given more economic security, people naturally start to limit their families, as has occurred in affluent countries in Europe and the U.S. However, unless the world changes its present unjust and inequitable social, political, and economic conditions, the world population will continue to grow, along with global problems of hunger, poverty, illiteracy, unemployment, and threats of violence.

There need be no inconsistency between Jewish survival and global survival, in terms of population growth. A Jew can have a large family and still help reduce famine and poverty in the world by working for conservation and justice. A family of five that has an impact equal to twenty people in India per person does far less harm (in terms of using resources and causing pollution) than a family of three with an impact equal to fifty Indians per person. A Jew who has few or no children can work for Jewish survival by striving to increase Jewish commitment through example, teaching, and writing.

The Jewish community should help provide support to those Jews who wish to have large families. Some mechanisms that the task force on Jewish population of the Commission on Synagogue Relations is exploring include:

- providing Jewish day-care facilities (these can be also used to educate and provide a social and psychological support system for Jewish children);
- providing child care during synagogue, Jewish center, and Y activities, to make it easier for young parents to be involved in Jewish and general community activities;
- providing scholarship help for larger families in Jewish schools;
- changing the dues structures of synagogues, Jewish centers, and Y's so that they do not penalize large families.[30]

There are additional ways that the Jewish community can work for Jewish survival besides exhorting Jews to have large families:

1. Providing programs to make Judaism more challenging and exciting. For example, involvement in some of the issues discussed in this book could entice many alienated Jews to return to Judaism and could reduce assimilation and intermarriage.

2. Improving Jewish education. Lower tuition rates at Jewish schools so that more children will attend.

3. Applying "physical fitness for Jewish survival." Teach Jews the benefits of nutritious meals and proper exercise and the importance of avoiding tobacco, alcohol (except in moderation, and especially as part of Jewish holy days), and drugs (other than those absolutely necessary medically).

Many ways in which Jews can work for better global conditions that would eventually lead to reduced population growth rates are discussed in "Action Ideas" in the appendix.

In summary, Jews can and should work for both Jewish and global survival. The two definitely need not be contradictory. While helping Jews who wish to have large families, the Jewish community should strive for a more meaningful, dynamic, committed, Jewish life and also work for a society that conserves resources, practices justice, seeks peace, and reduces hunger and poverty, thereby lessening people's need to have many children.

Chapter 13

Conclusion

*I am a Jew because the faith of Israel demands no abdication
of my mind.*
*I am a Jew because the faith of Israel asks every possible
sacrifice of my soul.*
*I am a Jew because in all places where there are tears and
suffering the Jew weeps.*
*I am a Jew because in every age when the cry of despair is
heard the Jew hopes.*
*I am a Jew because the message of Israel is the most ancient
and the most modern.*
I am a Jew because Israel's promise is a universal promise.
*I am a Jew because for Israel the world is not finished; men
will complete it.*
*I am a Jew because for Israel man is not yet fully created; men
are creating him.*
*I am a Jew because Israel places man and his unity above
nations and above Israel itself.*
*I am a Jew because above man, image of the divine unity,
Israel places the unity which is divine.*
—Edmond Fleg, "Why I Am a Jew"

What a wonderful path Judaism is!

Judaism worships a God who is the Father of all humanity, whose attributes of kindness, mercy, compassion, and justice are to serve as examples for all our actions.

Judaism teaches that every person is created in God's image and therefore is of supreme value.

Judaism asserts that people are to be co-workers with God in preserving and improving the earth. We are to be stewards of the world's resources and to see that God's bounties are used for the benefit of all. Nothing that has value can be wasted or destroyed unnecessarily.

Judaism stresses that we are to love other people as ourselves, to be kind to strangers, "for we were strangers in the land of Egypt," and to show compassion to the homeless, the poor, the orphan, the widow, even for enemies, and for all God's creatures.

Judaism places great emphasis on reducing hunger. A Jew who helps to feed a hungry person is considered, in effect, to have fed God.

Judaism mandates that we seek and pursue peace. Great is peace, for it is one of God's names, all God's blessings are contained in it, it must be sought in times of war, and it will be the first blessing brought by the Messiah.

Judaism exhorts us to pursue justice, to work for a society where each person has the ability to obtain, through creative labor, the means to lead a dignified life for himself and his family.

Judaism stresses involvement, nonconformity, resistance to oppression and injustice, and a constant struggle against idolatry.

There are four main themes discussed in this book:

1. The world faces many tremendous problems today: extensive poverty, threats to prime ecosystems, widespread hunger, nuclear weapons proliferation, shortages of resources such as energy, and rapid population growth.

2. Judaism has much to say about these issues. The application of Jewish values such as those related to pursuing justice, sharing resources, exhibiting kindness and compassion, loving our fellow human beings, working as partners with God in protecting the earth, seeking and pursuing peace, and in general imitating God are necessary to finding solutions to these problems.

3. Unfortunately, there has been a shift away from these basic Jewish values at a time when the world needs them more than ever before. There has been a political shift to the right in the Jewish community—a shift from prophetic values to chauvinistic values. There has been little effort to apply the Jewish tradition to the many critical problems that face the world today.

4. In the face of today's urgent problems, Jews must return to progressive Jewish values. We must remember our mission to be a light unto the nations, a holy people, a kingdom of priests, descendants of prophets, champions of social justice, eternal protesters against a corrupt, unredeemed world, dissenters against unethical systems. We must work for radical changes that will lead to a society where there is an end to oppression, hunger, poverty, and alienation. Jews must become actively involved in the missions of Jewish renewal and global survival.

141

The afternoon service for Yom Kippur includes the story of Jonah, who was sent by God to Nineveh to urge the people to repent and change their unjust ways in order to avoid their destruction. Today the whole world is Nineveh, in danger of annihilation and in need of repentance and redemption, and each one of us must be Jonah, with a mission to warn the world that it must turn from greed, injustice, and idolatry to avoid global oblivion.

Appendices

Appendix A

Action Ideas

It is not study that is the chief thing, but action.
—Kiddushin 40b

This book demonstrates that Jewish values can help solve many critical problems that face the world today. But, as the above quotation indicates, it is essential to *apply* these values, to put Jewish teachings into practice to help dislodge the world from its present apparent journey toward disaster.

First some preliminary considerations:

In attempting to change the world, sometimes we have to begin by changing ourselves. Rabbi Israel Salanter, the founder of the *mussar* (ethics) movement in Lithuania, taught: "First a person should put his house together, then his town, then his world."

If you feel that global crises are so great that your efforts will have little effect, consider the following. Our tradition teaches: "You are not obligated to complete the task, but neither are you free to desist from it" (Pirke Avot 2:21). We must make a start and do whatever we can to improve the world. As indicated in chapter 1, Judaism teaches that a person is obligated to protest when there is evil and, if necessary, to proceed from protest to action. Each person is to imagine that the world is evenly balanced between good and evil and that her or his actions can determine the destiny of the entire world.

Even if little is accomplished, trying to make improvements will prevent hardening of your heart and will affirm that you accept moral responsibility. Even the act of consciousness-raising is important because it may lead to future changes. Here are some things that each of us can do:

1. Become well informed. Learn the facts about global problems and related Jewish values from this and other books (see the bibliography).

2. Inform others. Wear a button. Put a bumper sticker on your car. Make up posters. Write timely letters to editors of local newspapers. Set up programs and discussions. Become registered with community, library, or school speakers' bureaus.
3. Simplify your life-style. Conserve energy. Recycle materials. Bike or walk whenever possible, rather than driving. Share rides. Use mass transit when appropriate.
4. Consider becoming a vegetarian. It is the diet most consistent with such Jewish values as showing compassion to animals, taking care of health, preserving the environment, sharing with hungry people, and conserving resources.
5. Work with groups on significant issues such as curbing the arms race, recycling resources, reducing dependence on nuclear energy, protecting human rights, funding human needs. If there are no local groups or if you differ with such groups on some important issue, such as Israel, set up a synagogue group.

   Names and addresses of Jewish groups working on these and similar issues are given in Appendix B.
6. Get books on global issues and Jewish responses into public and synagogue libraries. Donate your duplicates, request that libraries purchase such books, and/or, if you can afford it, buy some to donate.
7. Speak or organize events with guest speakers and/or audio-visual presentations showing how Jewish values relate to global issues.
8. Ask rabbis and other religious leaders to give sermons and/or classes showing how Judaism can be valuable in solving current problems.
9. Ask principals of Yeshivas and day·schools to see that their curricula reflect traditional Jewish concerns with peace and justice issues. Volunteer to speak to classes and help plan curricula.
10. Contact editors of local newspapers and ask that more space be given to global issues. Write articles and letters using information from this and similar books.
11. Try to change public policy with regard to the arms race, conservation, hunger, pollution, et cetera. Contact public officials. Organize letter-writing campaigns and group visits to politicians to lobby for a safer, saner, more stable world.
12. Consult with rabbis and religious educators or leaders on how to apply to today's critical issues such Jewish mandates as

"seek peace and pursue it," "*bal tashchit*," "justice, justice shalt
thou pursue," "love thy neighbor as thyself," and so on.

13. Consistent with Jewish teachings on helping hungry people
    and conserving resources, work to end the tremendous amount
    of waste generally associated with Jewish organizational func-
    tions and celebrations. Request that meat not be served, since
    production of meat wastes grain, land, and other resources;
    this also expresses compassion for the millions of people who
    lack an adequate diet.

14. Help set up a committee to reduce energy consumption in the
    synagogue. An excellent resource for this is *The Community
    Energy CARE-ing Handbook—An Activist's Guide for Ener-
    gizing Your Community toward Conservation and Renewable
    Energy,* by Leonard Rodberg and Arthur Waskow (see bibli-
    ography). Use steps taken to reduce synagogue energy use as
    a model for similar action on other buildings and homes.

15. Set up a social action committee in your synagogue or temple
    to help involve the group in educational and action-centered
    activities. Build coalitions with other social-justice-oriented
    groups in the community.

16. Raise the consciousness of your synagogue and other local
    Jewish organizations and individuals. Ask questions such as:

    - What would the prophets say about our society today?
      About Judaism in our time? About our synagogue activi-
      ties?
    - Where are the Jewish Ralph Naders crying out against
      "crime in the corporate suites" that leads to pollution, hun-
      ger, poverty, and waste of resources?
    - Why so few dreams of a better world through Jewish ideals?
    - Are we segregating God in our synagogues? If God is sanc-
      tified by justice and righteousness, why are we so compla-
      cent in the face of an unredeemed, immoral and unjust
      world?
    - Are we taking our ethical ideals and prophetic teachings
      seriously?
    - If we are implored "justice, justice, shalt thou pursue" and
      "let justice well up as waters and righteousness as a mighty
      stream," why the complacency regarding slums, poverty,
      police graft, corruption at all levels of government, and
      corporate malpractices that affect our health and safety?
    - Are we defining Jewish commitment too narrowly, in terms

147

of adherence to ritual only? Shouldn't Jewish commitment include sensitivity to moral and ethical values and social idealism?

- Have we forgotten who we are and what we stand for and Whom we represent? Have we forgotten our roles: to be a chosen people, a light unto the nations, a holy people, and descendants of the prophets (the original champions of social justice)?

If all Jews really put our splendid tradition into practice, can you imagine the effects? Would there be so much crime, violence, distrust, prejudice, discord, and air, water, and land pollution? Would we have so much "private affluence and public squalor"? Would we have the misguided priorities that lead to spending so many billions for bombs and not enough for human values and a better environment?

Appendix B

Jewish Peace and Social Action Groups

American Friends of Peace Now: P.O. Box 740, Radio City Station, New York, NY 10101.

Chai/Impact: 2027 Massachusetts Ave. NW, Washington, D. C. 20036. A grassroots network of Jews inspired by religious conviction to seek to influence U.S. public policy on many domestic and foreign policy issues, such as disarmament, the Middle East, economic justice, and human rights.

Givat Haviva Education Foundation: 150 Fifth Ave., Suite 1002, New York, NY 10011. Supports the work of the Kibbutz study center and educational-resource community.

International Center for Peace in the Middle East: 2 Karl Netter Street, Tel Aviv, Israel 65202.

Interns for Peace: 150 Fifth Avenue, Suite 1002, New York, NY 10011 (212) 255-8220. Aims to improve Arab-Jewish relationships in Israel and to improve standards of Arab health care, education, agriculture, and industry through Jewish and Arab interns working in Israeli villages.

Jewish Peace Fellowship: Box 271, Nyack, NY 10960. Believes that Jewish ideals and tradition provide inspiration for a nonviolent philosophy of life. Does extensive draft registration counseling.

OLAM, *The Religious Jewish Committee for Progressive Political Action:* c/o 210 Riverside Drive, Apt. lE, New York, NY, 10025. A group of halachically-observant Jews around North America who attempt to apply traditional Jewish values to current concerns and to act in the political world based on the Torah's communal and social ethics.

Oz V'Shalom: P.O. Box 4433, Jerusalem, Israel 91043. Religious Zionists in Israel who favor territorial compromise in order to establish peace, end Israeli occupation of Arab populations, and achieve the highest ideals and potentials of a new Israeli society.

Peace Now: P.O. Box 108, Jerusalem, Israel. Believes that rule over a million and a half Arabs distorts Jewish values and Zionist ideals. Urges Israeli government to take initiatives in seeking a compromise solution for peace.

Rainbow Sign: 7041 McCallum St., Philadelphia, PA 19119. A national Jewish nuclear disarmament organization, formed by Arthur Waskow, editor of *Menorah* magazine.

Religious Action Center of the Union of American Hebrew Congregations: 2027 Massachusetts Avenue, NW, Washington, D.C. The Reform movement's social action arm. Publishes materials and lobbies on many domestic and foreign policy issues.

The Shalom Center: Church Road and Greenwood Avenue, Wyncote, PA 19095. A national Jewish center wholly dedicated to the study, development, and public discussion of Jewish perspectives on preventing nuclear holocaust.

Grass-roots groups that are working to reduce poverty and hunger in the Jewish community include:
1) The Ark, 2341 West Devon Avenue, Chicago, IL 60659;
2) Project Dorot, 251 West 100th Street, New York NY, 10025;
3) Project Ezra, 197 East Broadway, New York, NY 10002.

Appendix C

Jewish Periodicals
That Discuss Global Issues

American Mizrachi Woman, Agatha Leifer (editor), 817 Broadway, New York, NY 10003.

Commentary, Norman Podhoretz (editor), 165 East 56th Street, New York, NY, 10022.

Congress Monthly, Nancy Miller (editor), 15 East 84th Street, New York, NY 10028.

Conservative Judaism, Harold Kushner (editor), 3080 Broadway, New York, NY 10027.

Genesis Two, Donald Perlstein (editor), 99 Bishop Allen Drive, Cambridge, MA 02139.

Hadassah Magazine, Alan M. Tigay (editor), 50 West 58th Street, New York, NY 10019.

Israel Horizons, Richard Yaffee (editor), 150 Fifth Avenue, New York, NY 10011.

Jewish Currents, Morris U. Schappes (editor), 22 East 17th Street (suite 601), New York, NY 10003.

Jewish Life, Rabbi Pinchas Stolper (editor), 45 West 36th Street, New York, NY 10018.

Jewish Peace Letter, Murray Polner and Carolyn Toll (editors), Jewish Peace Fellowship, Box 271, Nyack, NY 10960.

Jewish Spectator, Trude Weiss-Rosmarin (editor), P.O. Box 2016, Santa Monica, CA 90406.

Judaism, Robert Gordis (editor), 15 East 84th Street, New York, NY 10028.

Lilith, Susan Weidman Schneider (editor), 250 West 57th Street, New York, NY 10019.

Menorah, Arthur Waskow (editor), 7041 McCallum Street, Philadelphia, PA 19119.

Midstream, Joel Carmichael (editor), 515 Park Avenue, New York, NY 10022.

Moment, Leonard Fein (editor), 462 Boylston Street, Boston, MA 02116.

OLAM newsletter, Jonathan Wolf (editor), 210 Riverside Drive, Apt. 1E, New York, NY 10025.

Pioneer Women, Judith A. Sokoloff (editor), 200 Madison Avenue, New York, NY 10016.

Present Tense, Murray Polner (editor), 165 East 56th Street, New York, NY 10022.

Reconstructionist, Ira Eisenstein (editor), 31 East 28th Street, New York, NY 10016.

Reform Judaism, Aron Hirt-Manheimer (editor), 838 Fifth Avenue, New York, NY 10021.

Response, Steven M. Cohen (editor), 610 West 113th Street, New York, NY 10025.

Shalom, Murray Polner and Carolyn Toll (editors), Jewish Peace Fellowship, Box 271, Nyack, NY 10960.

Sh'ma, Eugene Borowitz (editor), Box 567, Port Washington, NY 11050.

Tradition, Rabbi Walter S. Wurzburger (editor), 1250 Broadway (Suite 802), New York, NY 10001.

Women's American ORT Reporter, Elie Faust-Levy (editor), 1250 Broadway, New York, NY 10001.

Women's League Outlook, Mrs. M. Milton Perry (editor), 48 East 74th Street, New York, NY 10021.

United Synagogue Review, Rabbi Marvin S. Weiner (editor), 155 Fifth Avenue, New York, NY 10010.

NOTES

Preface

1. Quoted in SANE (Committee for a Sane Nuclear Policy) slide show, "The Race Nobody Wins." SANE's address is 711G Street SE, Washington, D.C. 20003.
2. Paul Goodman, ed., *Seeds of Liberation* (New York: George Brazilier, 1964), p. 1.
3. Abraham Joshua Heschel, *The Insecurity of Freedom* (New York: Farrar, Strauss and Giroux, 1967), p. 218.

Chapter 1: Involvement and Protest

1. R. Judah Loew, *Netivot Olam, Shaar Hatochaha,* end of chapter 2.
    The result of failing to speak out against injustice is well expressed by the following statement by the German theologian Martin Niemoller:

> In Germany, the Nazis first came for the communists, and I didn't speak up because I was not a communist. Then they came for the Jews, and I did not speak up because I was not a Jew. Then they came for the trade unionists, and I didn't speak up because I wasn't a trade unionist.
>
> Then they came for me . . . and by that time, there was no one to speak up for anyone.

2. *Orchot Zaddikim 24* (Jerusalem: Eshkol 1967), p. 160; Rabbenu Yonah, *Sharei Teshuvah,* Shaar Sh'lishi, No. 5, 187 and 195.
3. American Jewish Congress, *Congress Bi-Weekly* 31/8 (May 11, 1964): 6.
4. Abraham Joshua Heschel, *The Insecurity of Freedom* (New York: Farrar, Straus and Giroux, 1967), p. 92.
5. *Judaism* 19 (1970): 38–58.
6. Abraham Joshua Heschel, *The Prophets* (Philadelphia: The Jewish Publication Society, 1962) and *The Insecurity of Freedom* (New York: Farrar, Straus and Giroux, 1967), pp. 9–13 and 92–93.
7. Norman Lamm, *The Royal Reach* (New York: Phillip Feldheim, Inc., 1970), p. 131.
8. "Why We Went," (paper of the Social Action Commission, Union of American Hebrew Congregations, New York).
9. Heschel, *The Prophets,* pp. 10–11.
10. Heschel, *Insecurity,* pp. 3–4.
11. "The Jerusalem Letter," *Gesher* 6, no. 2:2.
12. Samuel Chiel, *Spectators or Participants* (New York: Jonathan David, Pubs., Inc, 1969), p. 57.
13. Albert Vorspan and Eugene Lipman, *Justice and Judaism: The Work of Social Action* (New York: Union of American Hebrew Congregations, 1969), p. 231.

Chapter 2: Human Rights and Obligations

1. Maimonides, *Guide to the Perplexed,* part 2, chapter 54.
2. "The Last Days of Maimonides," in Abraham Joshua Heschel, *The Insecurity of Freedom (New York: Farrar, Straus, and Giroux, 1967), p. 291.*
3. Martin Buber, *Tales of the Hasidim, The Early Masters* (New York: Shocken Books, Inc., 1947), p. 227.
4. J. H. Hertz, *The Pentateuch and Haftorahs* (London: Soncino Press, 1958), p. 563.
5. Samuel Dresner, *Prayer, Humility, and Compassion* (Philadelphia: The Jewish Publication Society, 1957), p. 196.
6. Hertz, *The Pentateuch and Haftorahs,* p. 504.
7. Ibid.
8. Ibid.
9. There were several privileges that the stranger did not share. The cancellation of debts every Sabbatical year applied only to natives. While the Israelite was prohibited from charging a fellow-Israelite interest on loans, this was not applicable when the loan was to a non-Israelite. Also, a foreigner, if enslaved, did not enjoy the benefits of the law requiring the freeing of slaves every fifty years, at the time of the Jubilee.
10. Henry Cohen, *Justice, Justice: A Jewish View of the Black Revolution* (New York: Union of American Hebrew Congregations, 1968), pp. 51–52.
11. Many other statements by Jews of the Middle Ages indicated concern for the treatment of non-Jews by Jews. Levi b. Isaac ha-Hasid, a French Jew of the tenth century, stated:

    Treat with equal honesty the Christian as your brother in faith. If a Christian make a mistake to his loss, call his attention to it. If a Jew be a tax gatherer, he should demand no more from a Christian than from a Jew. A Jew shall not be untruthful in business with Jew or gentile.

    Rabbi Yehudah ben Samuel of Regensburg wrote in the *Sefer Hasidim:*

    Mislead no one through thy actions designedly, be he Jew or non-Jew. . . . Injustice must not be done to anyone whether he belongs to our religion or another.

    In his *Sefer Mitzvot Gedolot,* Moses ben Coucy wrote in 1245:

    Those who lie to non-Jews and steal from them belong to the category of blasphemers, for it is due to their guilt that many say the Jews have no binding law.

    These quotations are found in *Jew and Non Jew,* Tract No. 3, Popular Studies in Judaism, Union of American Hebrew Congregations, Cincinnati.
12. *Tradition* 8, no. 2 (Summer 1966).
13. Heschel, *Insecurity,* 86.
14. Ibid, p. 87.
15. Ibid, p. 93.
16. Ibid, p. 95.
17. M. Smilansky, "Fighting Deprivation in the Promised Land," *Saturday Review,* 15 October 1966, p. 185.

Chapter 3: Economic Justice

1. J. H. Hertz, *The Pentateuch and Haftorahs* (London: Soncino, 1957), p. 820. Rabbi Hertz also offers a Chassidic rabbi's interpretation of this Biblical verse: "Do not use unjust means to secure the victory of justice" (p. 820).

2. Rabbi Emanuel Rackman, "Torah Concept of Empathic Justice Can Bring Peace," *The Jewish Week,* 3 April 1977, p. 19.
3. Maimonides, *Mishneh Torah, Hilchot Matnot Aniyim,* 9:3.
4. Ibid, 7:10.
5. A whole section of the code of Jewish Law (Shulhan Arukh), Yoreh Deah 247–259, is devoted to the many aspects of giving charity. Some of the more important concepts are given below:

   247:1. It is a positive religious obligation for a person to give as much charity as he can afford.
   247:33: God has compassion on whoever has compassion on the poor. A person should think that, just as he asks of God all the time to sustain him and as he entreats God to hear his cry, so he should hear the cry of the poor.
   248:1: Every person is obliged to give charity. Even a poor person who is supported by charity is obliged to give from that which he receives.
   249:3: A man should give charity cheerfully and out of the goodness of his heart. He should anticipate in the grief of the poor man and speak words of comfort to him. But if he gives in an angry and unwilling spirit, he loses any merit there is in giving.
   250:1: How much should be given to a poor man? "Sufficient for his need in that which he wanteth" (Deuteronomy 15:8). This means that if he is hungry, he should be fed; if he has no clothes, he should be given clothes; if he has no furniture, furniture should be brought for him.

   According to the prophet Ezekiel, failure to help the needy led to the destruction of Sodom:

   Behold this was the iniquity of thy sister Sodom; pride, fullness of bread, and careless ease . . . neither did she strengthen the hand of the poor and needy . . . therefore I removed them when I saw it. . . .   (Ezekiel 16:49,50)

   A relationship between failure to help the poor and personal misfortune is emphasized in Proverbs 17:5, 21:13, and 28:27.
6. Genesis 18:2; Avot de Rabbi Nathan 7:17a,b.
7. Maimonides, *Mishneh Torah, Hilchot Shabbat* 2:3.
8. Samson R. Hirsch, *Horeb,* trans. Dayan Dr. I Grunfeld (London: Soncino, 1962), vol. 1, chapter 17, pp. 54–55.
9. Samuel Dresner, *Prayer, Humility, Compassion* (Philadelphia: Jewish Publication Society, 1953), p. 183.
10. In Judaism, there are just two limits to compassion. The first is that a judge must apply the law equally, without regard to persons. Only the strict rules of justice must apply. Second, one need not show compassion to those who lack compassion and practice cruelty. A Talmudic sage taught: "He who is compassionate to the cruel will, in the end, be cruel to the compassionate" (Yalkut, Samuel 121).
11. For a detailed study of the Jewish tradition on compassion for animals, see Noah J. Cohen, *Tsa'ar Ba'alei Hayim: The Prevention of Cruelty to Animals, Its Basis, Development, and Legislation in Hebrew Literature* (New York: Phillip Feldheim, Inc., 1976).

Chapter 4: Economic Democracy

1. Statement by Rabbi Abraham B. Bick, a disciple of Rabbi Abraham Isaac Kuk and a fighter for 'Jewish ethical socialism' in Poland in the early twentieth century, quoted in a thesis, *Religious Ethical Socialism: The Origins and Philosophy of the Jewish Religious Labor Movement,* by Max Bressler, Hebrew Union College, New York, Class of 1941.

1a. Richard Lichtman, *Toward Community* (Santa Barbara, California: Center for the Study of Democratic Institutions, 1966), p. 10.
2. Bressler, "Religious Ethical Socialism," p. 89.
3. *A Guide to the Kibbutz,* Tel Aviv, Israel (Ichud Habonim, 1960), p. 10.
4. China has apparently made some moves toward communal ownership of and control of land by those who work the fields. This has resulted in significant reduction in rural inequality; the income gap between the wealthiest and poorest in the rural population in China is now about one-fourth as great as in most Asian countries. While a dictatorship rules China at the national level, and there is repression and government intrusion at local levels, there is local involvement in planning in the communes.
5. Henry George, *Progress and Poverty,* abridged edition (New York: Robert Schalkenbeck Foundation, 1953).
6. This is discussed by Sidney E. Goldstein in *The Synagogue and Social Ethics* (New York: Block, Pubs. 1955), p. 337.
7. Ibid, p. 338.
8. Ibid, pp. 338, 339.
9. See "The Jewish Labor Movement and European Socialism" by Moshe Mishkinsky in H.H. Ben-Sasson and S. Ettinger, eds. *Jewish Society through the Ages* (New York: Schocken Books, Inc., 1971), pp. 284–96; and Irving Howe, *World of Our Fathers* (New York: Simon and Schuster, Inc., 1976), pp. 287–324.
10. Irving Howe and Kenneth Libo, eds., *How We Lived* (New York: Signet, 1981), p. 190.

Chapter 5: Ecology

1. Lester R. Brown, *The Twenty-ninth Day* (New York: W. W. Norton, 1978), p. 2.
2. Philip Nobile and John Deedy, eds., *The Complete Ecology Fact Book* (New York: Doubleday, 1972), p. 209.
3. Harold Holzer, "The Enemy Below," *New York* magazine, 7 February 1983, p. 43.
4. *Friends of the Earth* newsletter, 1982.
5. San Francisco Study Center, "The Ag Biz Tiller," (November 1976), No. 3: The San Francisco Study Center address is P.O. Box 5646, San Francisco, CA 94101.
6. Stephanie G. Harris and Joseph H. Highland, *Birthright Denied: The Risks and Benefits of Breast Feeding* (Washington, D.C.: The Environmental Defense Fund, 1977), pp. 2–13.
7. *The Economic Development of Colombia* (Baltimore: Johns Hopkins University Press, 1950), pp. 63 and 360.
8. Paul Flucke, "For the Sin of Terricide," in *New Prayers for the High Holy Days,* ed. Rabbi Jack Riemer (New York: Media Judaica, Inc., 1970), p. 44.
9. *The Global 2000 Report to the President* (New York: Penguin Books, 1982), pp. 1–3.
10. Philip Shabecoff, "Civilization's Folly: Million Species in Danger," The *New York Times,* 22 Nov. 1981.
11. See J. Cousteau, "The Oceans Are Dying," The *New York Times,* 14 Nov. 1971, and U.N. Document OPI/444-06208, April 1971.
12. *Israel Environment Bulletin* 3 (June 1976), 1:9.
13. Ibid, p. 7.
14. *State of Israel Yearbook,* 1973, p. 247.
15. Reprint of "Israel's Other Enemies" by Rochelle Saidel Wolk, *Women's American ORT Reporter,* Nov./Dec. 1980, p. 2.
16. Ibid.
17. Ibid, p. 4.
18. Ibid.

In order to combat the "unseen enemy" of pollution in Israel, a U.S. Committee for the Israel Environment has been set up. It has three primary functions:

- To provide an independent view on Israeli environmental issues;
- to provide an organizational structure to enable professional personnel to become actively involved in environmental projects of concern to Israel and to serve as clearinghouse for information of developments there; and
- to provide a broad base for Jews to participate in helping to solve Israel's environmental problems.

The group also brings Israeli environmentalists to the U.S. for training in modern techniques and educates people in the U.S. and Israel about Israel's environment. Further information about the committee's activities can be obtained by writing them at 511 Fifth Avenue, New York, NY 10017.

19. Story told by Rabbi Shlomo Riskin in "Biblical Ecology, a Jewish View," a documentary film, directed by Mitchell Chalek and Jonathan Rosen.
20. Some other statements in the Jewish tradition that reinforce the idea that the earth belongs to God include:

> Thine, O Lord, is the greatness, and the power, and the glory, and the victory, and the majesty, for all that is in the heaven and in the earth is Thine; . . . Both riches and honor come of Thee.
>
> 1 Chronicles 29:11,12

> Thus saith the Lord:
> The heaven is My throne,
> And the earth is My footstool;
> Where is the house that ye may build unto Me?
> And where is the place that may be My resting place?
> For all these things hath My hand made,
> And so all these things came to be,
> Saith the Lord.
>
> Isaiah 66:1,2

21. Samson Raphael Hirsch, *Horeb,* trans. Dayan Dr. I. Grunfeld (London: Soncino, 1962), vol. 2, chapter 56, p. 282.
22. Ibid, p. 280.
23. David Miller, *The Secret of Happiness* (New York: Rabbi David Miller Foundation, 1937), p. 9.
24. For a detailed analysis of how the misapplication of technology has been a prime cause of pollution problems, see Barry Commoner, *The Closing Circle* (New York: Bantam Books, 1974).
25. Wisconsin Department of Public Instruction, *Pollution: Problems, Projects, and Mathematics Exercises,* Bulletin No. 1082, p. 50.
26. S. R. Hirsch, "The Sabbath," in *Judaism Eternal,* edited and translated by I. Grunfeld (London: Soncino, 1956), pp. 22, 23.

Chapter 6: Hunger

1. Former Congressman Fred Richmond
1a. "World Hunger Facts," p. 2. This is available at Oxfam America's *Facts for Action,* 115 Broadway, Boston, MA 02116, p. 2.
2. Ibid.
3. Ibid.
4. Ibid.

5. "1981 World Population Data Sheet," Population Reference Bureau, Washington, D.C.
6. Pablo Neruda, excerpt from *The Great Tablecloth,* quoted in "World Hunger Facts."
7. *Philadelphia Inquirer,* 13 Oct. 1974, p. 9B.
8. Lester R. Brown, *In the Human Interest* (New York: Norton, 1974), p. 21.
9. Quoted in a paper on world hunger by Mazon, an ad hoc Jewish group which addressed hunger issues.
10. Class before Pesach (1978) given at the Young Israel of Staten Island.
11. "A Jewish Perspective," Directions '61 telecast, WABC-TV, January 1, 1961.
12. *Food First Resource Guide* (San Francisco: Staff of the Institute for Food and Development Policy, 1979, pp. 9–12. Also, for extensive discussions of the state of the world hunger, see: Susan George, *How the Other Half Dies: The Real Reasons for World Hunger* (Monclair, New Jersey: Allanheld, Osmun, and company, Pubs., Inc., 1977).
13. For more information on world population growth, see chapter 12 of this book and the various materials of the Population Reference Bureau, Washington, D.C.
14. China's progress in greatly reducing hunger is discussed in Frances M. Lappé and Joseph Collins, *Food First: Beyond the Myth of Scarcity* (Boston: Houghton, Mifflin Co., 1977), pp. 95–96, 166–67, and 400–401.
15. Congressional Budget Office, "Public Policy and the Changing Structure of American Agriculture," (September 1978), p. 27.
16. Study guide for filmstrip "Food First," p. 5. This is available at The Institute for Food and Development Policy, 1885 Mission Street, San Francisco, CA 94103.
17. *Report on 1960 Census of World Agriculture,* Food and Agriculture Organization.
18. U.S. Dept. of Agriculture, *Our Land and Water Resources,* Publication No. 1290 (1974), p. 32.
19. Council on Wage and Price Stability, Executive Office of the President. *Report on Prices for Agricultural Machinery and Equipment* (1976).
20. World Bank, *The Assault on World Poverty* (1975) p. 105.
21. Filmstrip, "Food First," study guide, p. 4.
22. *Unilever's World* (Washington, D. C.: Transnational Institute, 1975).
23. Lappé and Collins, *Food First,* p. 77.
24. For a detailed discussion of the effects of colonialism and neocolonialism, see Lappé and Collins, *Food First,* pp. 75–92.
25. *Food First Resource Guide,* p. 9.
26. Ibid.
27. Ibid, p. 21.
28. Ibid, p. 20.
29. Lappé and Collins, *Food First,* p. 16.
30. Ibid, p. 15.
31. Filmstrip "Food First" study guide, p. 7.
32. The wastefulness of the American meat-centered diet is extensively discussed by Frances M. Lappé, *Diet for a Small Planet* (New York: Ballantine, 1974).
33. Georg Borgstrom, *The Food and People Dilemma* (Belmont, California: Duxbury Press, 1973), p. 63.
34. Georg Borgstrom, "Present Food Production and the World Food Crisis," paper presented on September 2, 1974.
35. *New York Times,* 22 July 1975, p. 8.
36. *Food First Resource Guide,* p. 7.
37. P. Nobile and J. Deedy, *The Complete Ecology Fact Book,* (Garden City, N.Y.: Doubleday, 1972), p. 277.
38. "The Arms Race and World Hunger." This is available from Oxfam America's *Facts for Action,* 115 Broadway, Boston, Massachusetts 02116.
39. Ibid.
40. Ibid.
41. Ibid.

42. Ibid.
43. Arthur Simon, *Bread for the World* (New York: Paulist Press, 1975), p. 115.
44. Neville Maxwell, "Learning from Tacha," *World Development* 3 (July/August 1975), nos. 7 and 8.
45. Ronald J. Sider, *Rich Christians in an Age of Scarcity* (Downers Grove, Illinois: Intervarsity Press, 1977), p. 25.
46. Boyce Rensberger, "World Food Crisis: Basic Ways of Life Face Upheaval from Chronic Shortages," *New York Times,* 5 Nov. 1974.
47. Lester Brown, *By Bread Alone* (New York: Praeger, 1974), p. 206.

Chapter 7: Peace

1. For a detailed description and analysis of the arms race and its effects, see Ruth Leger Sivard, *World Military and Social Expenditures 1982* (Leesburg, Virginia: World Priorities, Inc., 1982), and her 1979, 1980, and 1981 reports.
2. Center for Defense Information, "Soviet Military Power: Questions and Answers," The *Defense Monitor* 11 (1982), 1:5.
3. Sivard, *World Military* (1982), p. 6
4. "Facing the Facts," Charts of the Traprock Peace Center, at Keets Road, Deerfield, Massachusetts 01342.
5. Ibid.
6. SANE flyer.
7. "U.S.-Soviet Military Facts," The *Defense Monitor* 11 (1982) 6:1.
8. Ibid, p. 3.
9. "World without Winners" slide show, SANE.
10. Robert L. Heilbroner, *An Inquiry into the Human Prospect* (New York: Norton, 1974), pp. 42–43.
11. "Facing the Facts."
12. Ibid.
13. Sidney Lens, *The Day Before Doomsday* (New York: Doubleday, 1977).
14. The *Bulletin of the Atomic Scientists,* 5801 S. Kenwood, Chicago, Illinois 60637.
15. "Facing the Facts."
16. "The New Generation of Nuclear Weapons," MARMIC, 1501 Cherry Street, Philadelphia, Pennsylvania 19102.
17. Sivard, *World Military (1981),* p. 14.
18. Sivard, *World Military (1982),* p. 5.
19. Ibid (1981), p. 6
20. Arthur Simon, *Bread for the World* (New York: Paulist Press, 1975), p. 122.
21. For discussions of how military spending affects human needs and economic conditions, see: Seymour Melman, *The Permanent War Economy* (New York: Simon and Schuster, 1974); The Boston Study Group, *The Price of Defense* (New York: Times Books, 1979); and Sivard, *World Military (1982),* pp. 14–29.
22. Quoted in SANE slide show, *"World without Winners."*
23. Simon, *Bread for the World,* p. 123.
24. Sivard, *World Military* (1978), p. 5.
25. Ibid.
26. "The Arms Race and World Hunger," Oxfam American Action Facts, 115 Broadway, Boston, Massachusetts 02116.
27. Ibid.
28. Sivard, *World Military (1982),* p. 9.
29. Council on Economic Priorities, based on Bureau of Labor Statistics.
30. Sivard, *World Military* (1982), p. 23.
31. *SANE World,* Committee for a Sane Nuclear Policy (July/August 1981), p. 1.
32. "Looting the Means of Production," *New York Times,* 26 July 1981, p. E21.
33. Quoted in "World Hunger," *World Vision* 19 (February 1975), p. 5.

34. *S.I. Advance* article by Susan Fogg (July 13, 1980), p. 1.
35. J. H. Hertz, *The Pentateuch and Haftorah* (London: Soncino, 1957), pp. 501, 502.
36. Samuel Belkin, *In His Image* (New York: Abelard-Schuman Limited, 1960), p. 227.
37. For a detailed comparison of U.S. and Soviet strength, see "American Strengths, Soviet Weakness," the *Defense Monitor* (June 1980) no. 5 and the *Monitor* 11, "Soviet Military Power: Questions and Answers" (1982), no. 1.
38. The *Defense Monitor* (June 1980), p. 4.
39. The *Defense Monitor* 11 (1982), 1:1.
40. Ibid, p. 2.
41. Ibid.
42. The *Defense Monitor* 9 (June 1980), 5:8.
43. The *Nation,* advertisement for new subscribers.
44. Marta Daniels, "The Soviet Threat—A Clear and Present Danger?" *AFSC,* no. 1, p. 5.
45. Ibid.
46. Ibid.
47. The *Defense Monitor* 9 (1982), 1:12.
48. Ibid, p. 6.
49. The *Defense Monitor* 11 (1982), 6:7.
50. William Sloane Coffin, "The Things that Make for Peace," in *Peace in Search of Makers,* ed. by Jane Rockman (Valley Forge, Pennsylvania: Judson Press, 1979), p. 138.
51. For an analysis of U.S. military aid to dictators, see Michael Klare, *Supplying Repression* (Washington, D. C.: Institute for Policy Studies, 1977).
52. American Friends Service Committee paper supporting a U.S.-USSR nuclear weapons freeze.
53. "Pentagon Rebuts Charges of U.S. Military Weakness," The *Defense Monitor* 9 (1981), 8A:1.
54. Daniels, "The Soviet Threat," p. 8.
55. Ibid.
56. Ibid.
57. Ibid.
58. *The Washington Spectator* 7 (May 1, 1981), 8:3.
59. Ibid.
60. *Synagogue Council of America News* (February 24, 1983).
61. See David Saperstein (ed.), *Preventing the Nuclear Holocaust—A Jewish Response* (New York: Union of American Hebrew Congregations, 1983), pp. 49–65; and Martin Ingall, ed., *Choose Life: Judaism and Nuclear Weapons* (Wyncote, Pennsylvania: The Shalom Center, 1983).

Chapter 8: Activism for Peace

1. Much of this chapter is based on material from Richard G. Hirsch, *Thy Most Precious Gift: Peace in Jewish Tradition* (New York: Union of American Hebrew Congregations, 1974).
2. Other Jewish statements that argue against reliance on power are:

>   The Egyptians are men, and not God;
>   And their horses are flesh, and not spirit.
>   When the Lord stretches out His hand,
>   The helper will stumble, and he who is helped will fall.
>   And they will all perish together.
>   Isaiah 31:3

A King is not saved by the multitude of a host;
A mighty man is not delivered by great strength.
A horse is a vain thing for safety;
Neither doth it afford escape by its great strength.

                                    Psalm 33:16–17

3. Maimonides, *Mishneh Torah*, Hilchot Melachim, 7:7.
4. J. C. Herold, *The Mind of Napoleon* (New York: Columbia University Press, 1955), p. 76.
5. See "Judaism and Peacemaking," *Fellowship*, Jan-Feb. 1976, pp. 14, 15.
6. Action Memo, Synagogue Council of America, January 1970, p. 1.
7. Shawn Perry, ed., "Words of Conscience, Religious Statements on Conscientious Objection," National Interreligious Service Board for Conscientious Objectors, Washington, D. C.
8. Ibid.
9. Ibid.

Chapter 9: Israel

1. Peace Now pamphlet, "Peace is Greater than Greater Israel" (October 1979), p. 1.
2. Everett Mendelsohn, *A Compassionate Peace—A Future for the Middle East* (New York: Hill and Wang, 1982), p. 117.
3. Ibid.
4. Ibid.
5. Ibid.
6. *New Outlook* (May 1982).
7. See Rabbi David Saperstein, "Judaism Demands Less Arms Spending," *Sh'ma* 7/130, (March 18, 1977), pp. 81–83.
8. Ruth Leger Sivard, *World Military and Social Expenditures, 1982* (Leesburg, Virginia: World Priorities, 1982), p. 28.
9. Mendelsohn, *A Compassionate Peace*, p. 26.
10. Oz V'Shalom poster.
11. *The Jewish Week*, 11 June 1978, p. 24.
12. "Our Faith Is a Faith of Life," an interview with Rabbi Ovadia Yosef, *New Outlook* (October 1979), p. 15.
13. " 'Not One Inch' Will Endanger . . . the Nation," an interview with Rabbi Jakobovits *New Outlook* (October 1979), p. 22.
14. Uriel Simon, "Spiritual and Political Dangers of Politicized Religion," *New Outlook*, (November 1978), p. 7.
15. *Shalom Network Newsletter* 3 (Spring 1983), 9:3.
16. Ibid.
17. Ibid.
18. Peace Now pamphlet, October 1979, p. 3.
19. Ibid, p. 4.
20. Ibid.
21. Ibid.
22. Ibid, p. 2.
23. *New York Times*, 20 May 1980, p. A10.
24. Mattityahu Peled, "Dissociating Israeli Security from More Territory," *New York Times*, 16 December 1977, op-ed article.
25. Peace Now pamphlet.
26. Rabbi Alex Schindler, president of the Union of American Hebrew Congregations, quoted in *Time*, 14 April 1980, p. 40.
27. *The Forward*, 22 July 1983, p. 19; and 29 July 1983, p. 19.

Chapter 10: International Relations

1. Lester Brown, *World without Borders* (New York: Vintage, 1973), p. 41.
2. "1983 World Population Data Sheet," Population Reference Bureau, Inc., Washington, D.C.
3. Ibid.
4. Ibid.
5. Ronald J. Sider, *Rich Christians in an Age of Hunger* (Downers Grove, Illinois: Intervarsity Press, 1979), p. 33.
6. Ibid. p. 35.
7. Ibid, p. 34.
8. Lester Brown, *In the Human Interest* (New York: Norton, 1974), p. 165.
9. "1983 World Population Data Sheet."
10. Robert L. Heilbroner, *The Great Assent: The Struggle for Economic Development in Our Time* (New York: Harper and Row, 1963), pp. 33–36.
11. "Sharing Global Resources," Script for slide show, NARMIC (research affiliate of the American Friends Service Committee), pp. 3–4.
12. James B. McGinnis, *Bread and Justice: Toward a New International Economic Order* (New York : Paulist Press, 1979), p. 32.
13. "Sharing Global Resources," p. 5.
14. Jim Wallis, *Agenda for Biblical People* (New York: Harper and Row, 1976), p. 85.
15. *Nicaragua and Central America Report* 1 (February 1980), no. 2.
16. "America and the World Revolution," quoted by David Horowitz, *Free World Colossus* (New York: Hill and Wang, 1971), p. 15.
17. *Common Sense* (November 1935), quoted by John M. Swomley, Jr., *American Empire* (New York: Macmillan Co., 1970), p. 150.
18. Ibid.
19. Ralph W. McGehee, *Deadly Deceits: My 25 Years in the CIA* (New York: Sheridan Square Publications, 1983), introduction.
20. For a comprehensive analysis, see Michael T. Klare, *Supplying Repression: U.S. Support for Authoritarian Regimes Abroad* (Washington, D.C.: Institute for Policy Studies, 1977).
21. McGuiness, *Bread and Justice,* pp. 39–54.
22. "Sharing Global Resources," p. 5.
23. Arthur Simon, *Bread for the World* (New York: Paulist Press, 1975), pp. 64–65.
24. *New York Times,* 11 July 1976, p. 3.
25. *New York Times,* 16 Aug. 1976, p. 2.
26. Theodore Morgan, *Economic Development: Concept and Strategy* (New York: Harper and Row, 1975), p. 205.
27. John P. Lewis and Valeriana Kallab, ed., *The United States and World Development, Agenda, 1982* (New York: Praeger, 1982), p. 228.
28. Ibid.
29. "1979 World Population Data Sheet," Population Reference Bureau, Inc., Washington, D.C.
30. Ibid.
31. Ibid.
32. Ibid.
33. Frances Moore Lappé and Joseph Collins, *Now We Can Speak* (San Francisco: Institute for Food and Development Policy, 1982), pp. 116–117.
34. *The Guardian,* 10 Aug. 1983, p. 27.
35. "Sharing Global Resources," p. 7.
36. Philip Goodman, (ed.), *The Sukkot and Simchat Torah Anthology* (Philadelphia, Pennsylvania: The Jewish Publication Society, 1973), p. 114.
37. Martin Buber, *Ten Rungs: Hasidic Sayings* (New York: Schocken, Books, Inc. 1961), p. 81.
38. Robert Gordis, "The Vision of Micha," in *Judaism and Human Rights,* ed. R. Konvitz, (New York: W. W. Norton, 1972), p. 287.
39. Ibid.

Chapter 11: Energy

1. Problems related to present energy policies are discussed in the following: Joseph Priest, *Energy for a Technological Society* (Reading, Massachusetts: Addison-Wesley, 1979), pp. 51–91; Barry Commoner, *The Poverty of Power* (New York: Bantam, 1977).
2. Ruth Leger Sivard, *World Energy Survey.* (Leesburg, Virginia: World Priorities, 1979), p. 5.
3. These two energy paths are discussed in *Soft Energy Paths: Toward a Durable Peace* by Amory B. Lovins (Washington, D. C.: Friends of the Earth International, 1977).
4. U.S. waste of energy is discussed in *Energy: The Case for Conservation,* (Worldwatch Paper 4), by Denis Hayes (Washington, D. C.: Worldwatch Institute, 1976), pp. 7–15.
5. Ibid, p. 14.
6. Ibid, pp. 20–25.
7. *The Good News About Energy,* Council on Environmental Quality, Washington, D. C.: 1979.
8. Robert Stobaugh and Daniel Yergin, ed. *Energy Future: Report of the Energy Project at the Harvard Business School* (New York: Ballantine, 1979).
9. *S. I. Advance* article, February 1981.
10. Pollution effects related to energy are discussed in *Energy for a Technological Society* by Joseph Priest, pp. 51–93.
11. Anna Gyorgy, ed., *No Nukes* (Boston: South End Press, 1979), p. 243.
12. Ibid.
13. Ibid.
14. V. E. Archer, J. D. Gillam, and J. K. Wagoner, "Respiratory Disease Mortality Among Uranium Miners" in *Annals, N.Y. Academy of Science,* p. 271.
15. Denis Hayes, *Rays of Hope: The Transition to a Post-Petroleum World* (New York: W. W. Norton, 1977), p. 71.
16. John H. Barton, "Intensified Nuclear Safeguards and Civil Liberties," NRC Contract No. AT (49-24-0190), October 31, 1975.
17. Additional Jewish statements about the importance and dignity of labor include:

When thou eatest the labor of thy hands,
Happy shalt thou be, and it shall be well with thee.
                    Psalms 128:2

Great is labor, for it honors he who performs it.
                    Nedarim 49b

Artisans are not required to stand up from their labor when a sage passes by.
                    Kiddushin 33a

A man is obliged to teach his son a trade and whoever does not teach his son a trade teaches him (in effect) to become a robber.
                    Tosefta Kidushin 1:11

Rabban Gamaliel, the son of Rabbi Judah the Prince said: Excellent is the study of Torah when combined with a worldly occupation, for the effort demanded by both makes sin to be forgotten.
                    Pirke Avot 2:2

Sweet is the sleep of a laboring man,
Whether he eat little or much,
But the satiety of the rich
Will not suffer him to sleep.
                    Ecclesiastes 5:11

The dignity of labor is raised to the highest level in a rabbinic dictum. It concerns the Holy of Holies, the repository for the Ark of the Covenant, the most sacred part of the central sanctuary. Only the high priest was permitted to enter, once a year on the Day of Atonement. The rabbinic statement reads:

> Great is work! Even the High Priest, if he were to enter the Holy of Holies on the Day of Atonement other than during the Avodah (worship service) is liable to death; yet for labor in it (for repair or mending), even those ritually unclean or blemished were permitted to enter (Mechilta).

Judaism considers all types of work to be dignified and ennobling, provided that through it an individual is participating in the creative process God intended for people: to improve the world. Consistent with this, the sages of Yavneh, the most famous Talmudical academy, stated:

> I am a creature, and my fellowman is a creature.
> I work in the city. He works in the fields.
> I rise early to go to my work.
> He rises early to go to his work
> Just as he does not feel superior in his work
> So I do not feel superior in mine.
> And if you should say that I do more for Heaven than he does,
> We have learned that it makes no difference.
> One may give more and one may give less,
> Providing that his intention is toward Heaven.
>
> Berachot 17a

18. Fact Sheet from Solar Lobby, 1001 Connecticut Ave., N.W., Washington, D.C. 20014. Also see the paper "Jobs and Energy," Environmentalists for a Full Economy, Washington, D. C.
19. See: Denis Hayes, *Energy: The Solar Prospect,* Worldwatch Paper 11 (Washington, D. C.: The Worldwatch Institute, 1977), p. 5.
20. CARE (Conservation and Renewable Energy) is discussed in *The Community Energy CARE-ing Handbook,* by Leonard Rodberg and Arthur Waskow (Washington, D. C.: Public Resource Center, 1980).

Chapter 12: Population Growth

1. Judith Zimmerman and Barbara Trainin, ed., *Jewish Population: Renascence or Oblivion* (New York: Federation of Jewish Philanthropies of New York, 1979), p. xiii.
2. Shirley Frank, "Population Panic—Why Jewish Leaders Want Jewish Women to Be Fruitful and Multiply," *Lilith,* Vol. 1, No. 4, Fall/Winter 1977, 8, p. 17.
3. The best source for current statistics on population is the Population Reference Bureau, 2213 M Street N.W., Washington, D. C. 20037. Their annual "World Population Data Sheet" is extremely valuable.
4. "1983 World Population Data Sheet," Population Reference Bureau, Inc., Washington, D.C.
5. Ibid.
6. Population Chart, Population Reference Bureau.
7. E. F. Schumacher, *Small is Beautiful* (New York: Harper and Row, 1973), p. 71.
8. "1983 World Population Data Sheet."
9. Ibid.
10. The group Zero Population Growth is located at 1346 Connecticut Avenue, N.W., Washington, D. C. 20036.

11. Negative Population Growth is located at 103 Park Avenue, New York, New York 10017.
12. David S. Shapiro, "Be Fruitful and Multiply," *Jewish Bioethics,* Fred Rosner and J. Bleich, ed. (New York: Sanhedrin Press, 1979), pp. 71,72.
13. Other statements in the Jewish tradition which show the great importance Judaism placed on raising a family include:

> To refrain from begetting is to impair the divine image.
> Genesis Rabbah 34:14

> Who brings no children into the world is like a murderer.
> Yebamot 63b

> A childless person is like one who is dead.
> Nedarim, 64b

> Was not the world created only for propagation?
> Hagiga, 2b

In his *Sefer Hamitzvot,* Maimonides comments on the purpose of the first *mitzvah:*

> God has commanded us to be fruitful and multiply with the intention of preserving the human species. . . .
> Commandment 212

The *Sefer Ha Chinuch* (Book of Training) also cites having children as a fundamental positive commandment, because without it, none of the other *mitzvot* could be fulfilled.
    The Talmud teaches that when one is brought to judgment, one of the first questions asked is "Did you undertake to fulfill the duty of procreation?" (Shabbat 31a). The importance of reproduction in order to populate the earth is also indicated by the prophet Isaiah (Isaiah 45:18):

> For thus says the Lord, the Creator of the heavens: He is God, He fashioned the earth and He made it, He has established it; He did not create it to be waste, He has fashioned it so that it will be inhabited.

14. Robert Gordis, "Be Fruitful and Multiply—Biography of a Mitzvah," *Midstream,* August/September 1983.
15. Steven M. Cohen, "The Coming Shrinkage of American Jewry," in Zimmerman and Trainin, *Jewish Population,* p. 3.
16. "The Jewish Family Facing Grave Crisis in the 1980's," Alvin I. Schiff, the *Jewish Week,* 22 October 1982, p. 3.
17. *Jewish Population,* p. viii.
18. The *Jewish Week,* 26 Nov. 1982, p. 5.
19. Frank, "Population Panic," p. 13.
20. Ibid, p. 13.
21. David M. Feldman, "Jewish Population: The Halachic Perspective," in *Jewish Population,* p. 42.
22. Frank, "Population Panic," pp. 12-17.
23. Ibid.
24. See Trude Weiss Rosmarin, "The Editor's Corner," the *Jewish Spectator* (Fall 1978), pp. 2–4.
25. Cohen, "Coming Shrinkage," p. 21.
26. Richard Yaffe, "Will Jews Disappear? Sociologist Remembers Past False Prophecies," the *Jewish Week,* 25 May 1979, p. 26.

27. Chaim Waxman, "How Many Are We? Where Are We Going?" *Jewish Life* (Spring/Summer 1982), p. 44.
28. Rashi's commentary on Genesis 41:50, based on Ta'anit lla.
29. Frances Lappé and Joseph Collins, *Food First* (Boston: Houghton Mifflin, 1977), p. 15.
30. *Jewish Population,* p. x.

Annotated Bibliography

A. Books Relating Judaism to Current Issues

Belkin, Samuel. *In His Image: The Jewish Philosophy of Man as Expressed in Rabbinic Tradition.* New York: Abelard-Schuman Limited, 1960.
The many ramifications in Jewish law of the concept that man is created in the image of God.

Cronbach, Abraham. *The Bible and Our Social Outlook.* New York: Union of American Hebrew Congregations, 1941.
The relations between Jewish ethical teachings and the correction of unjust conditions in society.

Dresner, Samuel H. *God, Man, and Atomic War.* New York: Little Books, Inc., 1966.
The relationship of the Jewish tradition to the world's most critical problem: the threat of atomic war.

Fisher, Rabbi Adam D. *". . . To Deal Thy Bread to the Hungry."* New York: Union of American Hebrew Congregations, 1975.
Analysis of Jewish views related to hunger, and modern *mitzvot* to help reduce it.

Gordis, Robert. *The Root and the Branch: Judaism and the Free Society.* Chicago: University of Chicago Press, 1962.
Shows revelance of the Jewish tradition to many moral issues of today.

Hertzberg, Arthur. *Great Religions of Modern Man: Judaism.* New York: Washington Square Press, Inc., 1963.
Biblical and traditional writings on the essential ideas of Judaism. An excellent reference to the great statements of the Jewish tradition.

Heschel, Abraham J. *The Insecurity of Freedom.* New York: Farrar, Straus and Giroux, 1967.
Superb set of essays relating Judaism to such issues as Jewish education, civil rights, Soviet Jewry, and Judaism in the diaspora.

———. *The Prophets.* Philadelphia: Jewish Publication Society, 1962.
Excellent analysis of history's greatest protestors against injustice.

Hirsch, Richard G. *The Way of the Upright—A Jewish View of Economic Justice.* New York: Union of American Hebrew Congregations, 1973.
Very good summary of Jewish ethical teachings related to economic behavior.
———. *There Shall Be No Poor.* New York: Union of American Hebrew Congregations, 1965.
The application of the Jewish concern for economic justice to the problem of poverty.
———. *Thy Most Precious Gift, Peace in Jewish Tradition.* New York: Union of American Hebrew Congregations, 1974.
An excellent source for traditional Jewish views on war/peace issues.

Ingall, Martin, ed. *Choose Life: Judaism and Nuclear Weapons.* Wyncote, Pa.: The Shalom Center, 1983.
An anthology of articles, interviews, speeches and sermons concerning Judaism and nuclear weapons.

Jacobs, L. *What Does Judaism Say About . . . ?* New York: New York Times Books, 1973.
What Judaism says about many topics, including justice, charity, peace, vegetarianism, and civil disobedience.

Jung, Leo. *Human Relations in Jewish Law.* New York: Board of Jewish Education, 1970.
A "pioneering effort by a renowned rabbi-scholar to describe suc-

cinctly the traditional sources from which Jewish communal services have drawn their inspiration through the many centuries of Jewish community life. . . . A *halacha* of Social Service" (from the foreword to the book).

Kellner, Menachem Marc, ed. *Contemporary Jewish Ethics*. New York: Sanhedrin, 1978.
Has sections on political ethics, civil disobedience, pacifism, capital punishment, and business ethics.

Konvitz, R., ed. *Judaism and Human Rights*. New York: W. W. Norton, 1972.
A collection of essays, mainly by contemporary Jewish scholars, relating the Jewish tradition to such issues as human rights, ecology, peace, and freedom.

Lamm, Norman, ed. *The Good Society*. New York: Viking, 1974.
A survey of Jewish material related to Jewish teachings on such issues and concepts as compassion, charity, ethics, and peace.
———. *The Royal Reach: Discourses on the Jewish Tradition and the World Today*. New York: Feldheim, 1970.

Levine, Aaron. *Free Enterprise and Jewish Law—Aspects of Jewish Business Ethics*. New York: Ktav, 1980.

Meyerowitz, Arthur. *Social Ethics of the Jews*. New York: Bloch, 1935.
Many quotations showing the Jewish view on such issues as justice, charity, peace, and compassion.

Miller, Rabbi David. *The Secret of Happiness*. New York: Committee of Rabbi David Miller Foundation, 1937.
The many applications of the Jewish concept of "acts of loving kindness."

Polner, Murray, ed. *The Disarmament Catalogue*. New York: Pilgrim Press, 1982.
Valuable collection of articles, stories, and cartoons related to the arms race.

Rackman, Emanuel. *Jewish Values for Modern Man*. New York: Jewish Educational Committee, 1962.
Jewish traditional views on current issues, presented with a scholarly approach.

Saperstein, Rabbi David, ed. *Preventing the Nuclear Holocaust—A Jewish Response*. New York: Union of American Hebrew Congregations, 1983.
Excellent material on Jewish responses to the nuclear arms race.

Schwartz, Richard H. *Judaism and Vegetarianism*. Smithtown, Long Island: Exposition Press, 1982.
Argues that Jewish mandates to show compassion to animals, preserve health, help feed the hungry, preserve the earth, and pursue peace point to vegetarianism as the ideal diet.

Strassfeld, Sharon and Michael. *The Third Jewish Catalog—Creating Community*. Philadelphia: Jewish Publication Society, 1980.
Has sections on social justice, ecology, and compassion for animals.

Vorspan, Albert and Eugene J. Lipman. *Justice and Judaism*. New York: Union of American Hebrew Congregations, 1956.
Jewish tradition on housing, employment, education, peace, and other political issues.

Vorspan, Albert. *Great Jewish Debates and Dilemmas, Jewish Perspectives on Moral Issues in Conflict in the Eighties*. New York: Union of American Hebrew Congregations, 1980.
Fine discussion of controversial issues facing the Jewish community and the world, such as energy, ecology, economic justice, zero population growth, and race relations.

Waskow, Arthur I. *Godwrestling*. New York: Schocken Books, Inc., 1979.
Excellent application of Jewish tradition to "wrestle" with current problems such as injustice and violence.
———. *These Holy Sparks, The Rebirth of the Jewish People*. San Francisco: Harper and Row, 1983.
The views of a radical Jew on Israeli and American political and ethical issues.

B. Books Relating General Religious Values to Current Issues

Ahmann, Mathew, ed. *Race: Challenge to Religion*. Chicago: Henry Regnery, 1963.

Byron, William. *Toward Stewardship, An Interim Ethic of Poverty, Pollution, and Power.* New York: Paulist Press, 1975.

McGinnis, James B. *Bread and Justice, Toward a New International Economic Order.* New York: Paulist Press, 1979.
Advocates a new international economic order to eliminate global poverty and hunger.

Wallis, Jim. *Agenda for Biblical People—A New Focus for Developing a Life-Style of Discipleship.* New York: Harper and Row, 1976.
Criticizes "establishment religion" and emphasizes the need to return to the radical message of the Bible.

C. Articles Relating Judaism and Current Issues

1. Hunger

Gruber, Mayer, I. "Is Buying from Nestle a Sin for Jews?" *Sh'ma* 9/178 (October 5, 1979), pp. 2–4.

Harris, Carrie, "Synagogue Action on Hunger: A Passover-Shevuoth Model." Paper prepared for the American Friends Service Committee, 15 Rutherford Place, New York, New York 10003.

Pilchik, Rabbi Ely. "Judaism and World Hunger." Paper delivered to Metropolitan Council of Union of American Hebrew Congregations (November 2, 1975), Temple Sinai, Summit, New Jersey.

Robinson, Michael A. "World Hunger, the Torah, and Us," *Keeping Posted* 20/6 (March, 1975), pp. 3–6.

Synagogue Council of America. "Resolution on World Hunger," Adopted by the Plenum of SCA on January 8, 1975.

2. Ecology

Carmell, Aryeh. "Judaism and the Quality of the Environment." In *Challenge: Torah Views on Science and Its Problems,* edited by Aryeh Carmell and Cyril Domb. London: Feldheim, 1976, pp. 500–525.

Gordis, Robert. " 'The Earth Is the Lord's—Judaism and the Spoliation of Nature," *Keeping Posted* 16/3 (December 1970), pp. 5–9.

Helfand, Jonathan, I. "Ecology and the Jewish Tradition: A Postscript," *Judaism* 20/3 (Summer 1971), pp. 330–35.

Lamm, Norman. "Ecology in Jewish Law and Theology" in *Faith and Doubt*. New York: Ktav, 1971, pp. 162–85.

Pelcovitz, Rabbi Ralph. "Ecology and Jewish Theology," *Jewish Life* 37/6 (July–August 1970), pp. 23–32.

Turk, Rabbi Samuel A. "Thou Shalt Not Destroy," *Jewish Life* (October 1972), pp. 13–18.

Vorspan, Albert. "The Crisis of Ecology: Judaism and the Environment." Chapter in *Jewish Values and the Social Crisis,* New York: Union of American Hebrew Congregations, 1970.

3. Peace

"Judaism and Peacemaking," the entire issue of *Fellowship* 42 (Jan.-Feb. 1976), No. 1–2.

The Jewish Peace Fellowship (Box 271, Nyack, NY 10960) has a variety of booklets and pamphlets, including *Can a Jew Be a CO?*, *The Roots of Jewish Nonviolence, A Service for Survival,* and *Peace in the Bible.*

Subject Index

Index of Biblical Passages